THE IMPORTANCE OF RURAL LIFE
ACCORDING TO THE
PHILOSOPHY OF ST. THOMAS AQUINAS
A STUDY IN ECONOMIC PHILOSOPHY

BY
GEORGE H. SPELTZ, M.A.
PRIEST OF THE DIOCESE OF WINONA

Nihil Obstat:

GULIELMUS J. McDONALD, Ph.D.
Censor Deputatus
Washingtonii, D.C., die 19 Maii, 1944.

Imprimatur:

✠LEO BINZ
Episcopus Pinarensis
Administrator Apostolicus Ecclesiae Winonensis

Datum Winonae, die 23 Maii, 1944.

To My Father and Mother
On Their Fortieth Wedding Anniversary

ABBREVIATIONS TO THOMISTIC WORKS

In Polit.—Commentary of St. Thomas on Aristotle's *Politics.*

In Ethic.—Commenary of St. Thomas on Aristotle's *Nicomachean Ethics.*

Cont. Gent., III, 135—*Summa Contra Gentiles,* Book III, chapter 135.

S. T., Ia, q. 50, art. 1, ad 1—*Summa Theologica, prima pars,* question 50, article 1, answer to the first objection.

S. T., Ia-IIae—*Summa Theologica, prima secundae.*

S. T., IIa-IIae—*Summa Theologica, secunda secundae.*

S. T., IIIa—*Summa Theologica, tertia pars.*

In Sent. II, d. 17, q. 3, art. 2, ad 7—Commentary of St. Thomas on the *Sentences of Peter the Lombard,* Book II, distinction 17, question 3, article 2, answer to the seventh objection.

De Reg. Princ., I, 14—*De Regimine Principum,* Book I, chapter 14.

De Pot., q. VI, art. 3, c.—*Quaestiones Disputatae, De Potentia,* question VI, article 3, body of the article.

TABLE OF CONTENTS

Table of Contents

Table of Contents

PREFACE

In the traditional treatment of Thomistic thought agrarian matters have been given little, if any, formal consideration in separate studies. Hence it is to be expected that some, confronted with the title of this dissertation, will be inclined to ask whether the Angelic Doctor gave any thought to agrarian problems, and whether he worked out an agrarian philosophy.

While such questions will undoubtedly be asked, it is hoped to demonstrate here that there is equal, or stronger, reason to ask the same questions with the underlying assumption turned about. There is more reason to assume that Aquinas concerned himself with agrarian matters than that he did not. These matters are the philosopher's concern, whose task it is, according to Aristotle, to order things. More particularly it is the duty of the social philosopher to further good order within the economic and social relations of men. The land is fundamental. If people are not well ordered in their use of it, it will be of little avail to try to order them in other economic and social matters. The great social philosophers, both before and after Aquinas, have realized this and accordingly have given much attention to the problem in their political economies. For Aristotle there was a close connection between natural wealth-getting from the land and the "good life". The Physiocrats in France and Adam Smith in England gave careful and lengthy consideration to agrarian problems in their political economies. This is to mention only a few. Did then St. Thomas, who lived in an age when the larger part of the economic and social life of the people was carried on in immediate relation to the land and its institutions, fail to include in his comprehensive philosophy the principles by which people might be well ordered in their relation to each other, in matters pertaining to the land? The presumption would seem to be that St. Thomas did treat these matters, and we should therefore have much reason to be surprised if we should find that he had nothing important to say, either directly or by implication, on the rural life. But this reasonable presumption, if it existed, has not been acted upon. Of the great number of studies on St. Thomas none has been found that purports to examine his system for the principles of a sound agrarian economic philosophy. This gives the hope that the present study is not only justified but seemingly overdue.

The whole method of this study has aimed to bring to bear upon the pressing socio-economic problems of today, not practices from Medieval times, but rather principles from Aquinas' philosophy. The carrying over of the former would represent retrogression; the application of the latter can bring true progress. With this in mind an historical background is included in this study and against this background is exposed the Thomistic teaching from a critical examination of pertinent texts. The principles thus discovered are analyzed and applied to the contemporary situation, account being taken of the change in conditions and the causes responsible for it. A careful analysis of these causes is made in order to separate those that have arisen due to a natural progress in the technique of securing material human needs from those that are due to the injection of a false philosophy, whether in good faith or in bad faith, into agrarian life. When this has been done it is more evident that Aquinas' sound agrarian principles are important for the good order of his entire philosophical system and the good order of his times, and that they have, as well, a contribution to make today.

The adherents of the agrarian-decentralist movement now flourishing in this country have done much towards raising and solving the socio-economic problems confronted in this study. It is our hope to add to the work of this movement by clarifying the relevant principles that give direction to its investigations and factual findings. Unless Thomistic philosophy can give such assistance then there is little reason for calling it the *philosophia perennis.*

The first chapter of this study is offered as a general survey of those principles of Thomistic philosophy which touch upon the rural life. Apology is made for any repititions in later chapters of subject matter necessarily anticipated in the general survey of the first chapter. An attempt has been made to keep these at a minimum. As the title of this dissertation suggests, this is a general study. Its purpose is to open up this particular field of agrarian economic philosophy by giving, with the aid of Thomistic principles, as balanced a presentation as possible of the problems involved. Since the limits of this study will not allow for a thorough solution of the many problems that will present themselves, it is hoped that others may find it worth their while to take up these problems individually and subject them to a more penetrating philosophical analysis.

During the period of preparation of this dissertation the author has been deeply grateful to the many who have helped him in this work. He wishes here particularly to express sincere thanks to His Excellency, the Most Rev. Francis M. Kelly, D. D., Bishop of Winona, and to His Excellency, the Most Rev. Leo Binz, D. D., Coadjutor Bishop of Winona and Apostolic Administrator, for the opportunity to pursue graduate study at the Catholic University of America. The writer recalls with gratitude the constant encouragement and assistance which he received during the last three years from the Rev. Doctor William J. McDonald who suggested this study and gave liberally of his time and thought to its supervision. He is thankful to the Dean of the School of Philosophy, the Very Rev. Doctor Ignatius Smith, O.P., for creating that atmosphere of scholarship and friendliness which has become a mark of this School of the University. He is also grateful to him and to the Rev. Doctor John K. Ryan for their careful reading of

Preface

the manuscript and for suggestions. He wishes to thank all the teachers at the University under whom he was privileged to study. He extends his thanks beyond the University to the Right Rev. Msgr. Luigi G. Ligutti, Executive Secretary of the National Catholic Rural Life Movement, and to Doctor O. E. Baker of the University of Maryland, who have given inspiration through their work with the Rural Life Movement and who have in other ways helped him.

CHAPTER I

THE GENERAL BEARING OF THOMISTIC PHILOSO-
PHY ON RURAL LIFE

In the course of this study there will often be occasion to speak of the "agrarian philosophy" of St. Thomas Aquinas. In so far as he devotes no special *opusculum* to this subject, nor does he in any one place give it a formal and complete treatment, it will be necessary to formulate a working definition of this phrase under which may then be grouped all those Thomistic principles relevant to the present investigation. By agrarian philosophy will be understood that science which, with a view to the "good life",[1] orders man in his use of the land. Guided by this definition, the present introductory chapter undertakes an examination of Aquinas' teaching on man, both as an isolated individual

---

[1] The phrase, "good life", is taken from Aristotle, *Polit.*, Bk. I, chap. 8, 1256 b, 32-3: "The amount of property which is needed for a good life is not unlimited." Also Bk. I, chap. 2, 1252 b, 30: "When several villages are united in a single complete community, large enough to be nearly or quite self-sufficing, the state comes into existence, originating in the bare needs of life, and continuing in existence for the sake of a good life." St. Thomas also uses the phrase, and lays down two requirements for the good life: the first is to act in a virtuous manner; the second is a sufficiency of bodily goods. Cf. *below*, chap. III, 1, and *De Reg. Princ.*, I, 15. Where Aristotle states that the end of the state is the "good life," St. Thomas writes that the end of society is to bring men through virtuous living in this mortal life, to final beatitude after death in the enjoyment of God. Cf. *below*, chap. III, 1, and *De Reg. Princ.*, I, 15. In the above definition of agrarian philosophy, according, the phrase "good life," will be taken to mean virtuous living in this mortal life—one condition of such living being a sufficiency of bodily goods—ordered to beatitude after death.

1

for whom there is a fixed hierarchy of values set by the order of reason, and as a political and social animal who must cooperate with others in an ordered manner for the attainment of these values, whether spiritual or material. In this manner it will be possible to learn what constitutes, according to the mind of Aquinas, the "good life", and to what degree this is attainable through the rural life.

1. THE PLACE OF MATERIAL GOODS

According to the Angelic Doctor the "good life" involves other values[2] besides the spiritual. In this he stands opposed to any philosophy such as that of the Stoics. In the *Summa Theologica* he finds occasion in one passage to give their position on this point and to refute it. Rejecting bodily goods as true goods for man, the Stoics held that virtue is man's only good. From this they derived the further conclusion that the only evil that could befall man is vice and consequently, if he were virtuous, then no evil whatsoever 'could befall him or cause him sorrow. St. Thomas, basing his teaching on a different conception of man, rejects their line of argument. Man, he affirms, is composed of body as well as of soul. Accordingly, anything that helps to conserve the life of man represents a good for him. Man, by the same token, is subject to other evils besides vice. Even though he be virtuous he can yet suffer evil through the lack of bodily goods; and having fallen into this evil he will be sorrowful.[3]

---

[2]Cf. Ward, Leo Richard, C. S. C., *Philosophy of Value*, dissertation submitted to the Faculty of Philosophy of the Catholic University of America, New York: Macmillan, 1930, especially chap. VIII, for a general treatment of the problem of value.

[3]Cf. *S.T.*, Ia-IIae, q. 59, art. 3, c: Nullum autem malum existimant (stoici) posse accidere sapienti. Crediderunt enim, quod, sicut solum hominis bonum est virtus, bona autem corporalia nulla bona hominis sunt; ita solum inhonestum est hominis malum, quod in vir-

a) The Philosopher's Concern with Them

It pertains to the philosopher to be concerned with these material needs of man. Commenting upon the *Politics* of Aristotle, St. Thomas writes that it belongs to the philosopher to be concerned with such subjects as the natural wealth-getting of the husbandman. Moreover, he is to concern himself with this function not only in its theoretical aspects but also in its practical considerations, such as the knowledge of livestock and of tillage. These matters take on a certain dignity and become subjects of the philosopher's consideration because they are related to human needs.[4] St. Thomas goes beyond Aristotle in this matter. Aristotle had said that a discussion of the "practical part" of wealth-getting was "not unworthy of philosophy, but to be engaged in them practically is illiberal and irksome."[5] Commenting upon these words Aquinas writes in agreement with the Philosopher that "it is easy to consider these things in a general way," adding however that, "it is necessary to have an experiential knowledge of these things, to this end that man may make as perfect a use of them as possible."[6] There is here the suggestion—at least by silence—that St. Thomas repudiates the implication left by Aristotle that manual work is "illiberal and irksome," if not degrading. In a later chapter[7] it will be shown that St. Thomas does not regard it as unbecoming for man to

---

tuoso esse non potest. Sed hoc irrationabiliter dicitur: cum enim homo sit ex anima et corpore compositus, id quod confert ad vitam corporis conservandam, aliquod bonum hominis est; non tamen maximum, quia eo potest homo male uti: unde et malum huic bono contrarium in sapiente esse potest; et tristitiam moderatam inducere.

[4] Cf. *In Polit.*, I, 9, princ.: omnia enim hujusmodi, quae pertinent ad operationes humanas, habent liberam, idest expeditam contemplationem.

[5] *Politics* Bk. I, chap. 11, 1258b, 9-12.

[6] *In Polit.*, I, 9, princ.: quia facile est ea considerare in universali; sed tamen necesse est quod habeatur experientia circa ipsas, ad hoc quod homo possit perfectum usum eorum habere.

work with the material goods of this earth in order that they may serve the purpose for which they were created—human needs—as perfectly as possible.

Among the works of St. Thomas is one which is an important source of his agrarian philosophy, namely, a letter to Hugh, King of Cyprus, sent to him for the education of his son.[8]   From this work, in which Hugh is advised in much detail about the founding of a city, it is evident that the Angelic Doctor has interested himself in the material needs of man.   An adequate provision of material goods is necessary for the practice of virtue, and consequently the King must interest himself in these matters.[9]

b) Bodily Goods and External Goods or Riches

St. Thomas insures against an overemphasis of bodily goods by calling them "instrumental."[10]   That they are only instrumental, no one today would deny, at least not in theory.   In practice, however, modern man has become inordinately preoccupied with them.   As Pope Pius XI pointed out:

> The condition of the economic world today lays more snares than ever for human frailty. For the uncertainty of economic conditions and of the whole economic regime demands the keenest and most unceasing straining of energy on the part of those engaged therein. . . .Easy returns, which a market unhampered by laws offers to any one, lead many to interest themselves in trade and

---

[7]Cf. *below*, chap. III.

[8]*De Regimine Principum*, transl. by G. B. Phelan, *On the Governance of Rulers*, Toronto: Institute of Medieval Studies, and New York: Sheed and Ward, 1938.   The translation covers only the first book and the first four chapters of the second book which are the certainly authentic parts of the work.

[9]Cf. *op. cit.*, I, 15.

[10]Cf. *op. cit.*, Bk. I, chap. 15; *S.T.*, IIa-IIae, q. 58, art. 10, ad. 2.

exchange, their one aim being to make clear profits with the least labor.[11]

The Thomistic synthesis provides against this disorder by pegging material goods into a fixed place within the hierarchy of man's needs. This is achieved in part, by relegating them as means to an end that is outside and above them, to an end that is fixed and capable of controlling them. It is on the basis of a consideration of ends that St. Thomas divides material goods. Those that pertain to the conservation of an individual, i.e., those that are immediately ordered to a fundamental need of the body, as food and drink, are called goods of the body *(bonum corporis)*; those that are not ordered to any such strict need of the body, but are only ordered in a general way to human needs, fall into the class of external goods *(bonum exterius)*. Such are riches *(divitiae)*.[12] Of these two classes of material goods, those called "bodily goods" are the higher because necessary for the practice of virtue.[13] Moreover, the amount of these necessary for the practice of virtue, and consequently for the good life, is strictly limited, a truth emphasized both by Aristotle and by Aquinas.[14] On the other hand, external goods, namely riches, inasmuch as they are ordered only in a general manner to human needs, are not regarded as essential for "an act of virtue." Since riches are sought

---

[11]Pius XI, encyclical letter, *Quadragesimo Anno*, New York: The America Press, 1938, p. 37.

[12]Cf. *S.T.*, Ia-IIae, q. 84, art. 4, c. for St. Thomas' threefold division of goods, with the second and third pertaining to material goods: bonum autem hominis est triplex: est enim primo quoddam bonum animae, quod scilicet ex sola apprehensione rationem appetibilitatis habet, sicut excellentia laudis vel honoris....Aliud est bonum corporis, et hoc vel pertinet ad conservationem individui, sicut cibus et potus...aut conservationem speciei sicut coitus...Tertium bonum est exterius, scilicet divitiae. Cf. also, *S.T.*, Ia-IIae, q. 2, art. 1, c, for the division of riches into natural and artificial.

[13]Cf. *De Reg. Princ.*, I, 15.

[14]Cf. Aristotle, *Polit.*, Bk. I, chap. 8, 1256b, 35; *In Polit.*, I, 8.

for their power to procure other things rather than for the direct satisfaction of some bodily need, they easily come to be desired inordinately. Of those who are given to this inordinate desiring Aristotle writes that they, not knowing how to live well, think that enjoyments must be had in excess. For this they need an excess of riches.[15] As a result of this inordinate desire for riches man is unduly preoccupied with the quest for material goods, failing to realize, as St. Thomas points out, that riches are the least among human goods—less than the goods of the body, less than the goods of the soul, less than the divine good.[16]

c) Agrarian Institutions as a Check on Undue Emphasis upon Riches

Guided by this scale of values, St. Thomas gives an eminent place in the hierarchy of human activities to the life of the husbandman,[17] whose work is ordered to the procuring of bodily goods for the immediate use of the household. Since the need of any one household for natural wealth, such as food and clothing, is limited, so also the activity of the husbandman, as long as it was directed to the procuring of bodily goods and not of external goods primarily, was proportionately limited and tended less to become inordinate. It was comparatively easy in the agrarian way of life advocated by Aristotle and Aquinas, for the people to retain a true evaluation of bodily goods, as opposed to external goods, the former having a fixed relation to the needs of the various households. They were educated to a true sense of value through the prevailing practice of the institu-

---

[15]Cf. Aristotle, *Polit.*, Bk. I, chap. 9, 1258a, 5; *In Polit.*, I, 8.

[16]Cf. *S.T.*, IIa-IIae, q. 118, art. 5, c: bonum autem exteriorum rerum est infimum inter humana bona; est enim minus quam bonum corporis, quod etiam minus est quam bonum animae, quod exceditur a bono divino.

[17]Cf. *In Polit.*, I, 8.

tions of the time. While husbandry was sufficiently prevalent as an activity conjoined to household management,
there was far less danger that external goods should rise to
the unwarranted place of becoming a dominant end in themselves, with a consequent disorder in human affairs.

As a corollary of their teaching on the secondary place
of external goods, both Aristotle and Aquinas warned
against the practice of trading. Because of the latent greed
in men, those who traded might easily fall into the practice
of trading for the purpose merely of amassing external
goods. Such trading would be directed to the unnatural and
limitless end of amassing money, ever more money. This
is to exalt external goods *(bonum exterius)* to the status of
ends in themselves; it is to upset the ordered hierarchy of
values. However, not all trade is to be discouraged. Some
trade is needed to effect a distribution of goods and to
prevent waste where goods of any one kind are in abundance; but this trading should be limited. "The perfect city
will make a moderate use of merchants."[18]

Modern scholars have pointed out an error springing
from the sixteenth century, the influence of which persists
today. The idea that an abundance of earthly riches may
be taken as a sign of God's favor and of predestination has
tended to encourage the latent greed in men that Aristotle
and Aquinas has sought in various ways to control. This
idea has in part been responsible for an exaggerated capitalistic spirit.[19] Where such an idea has a vogue, even in a
modified degree, the rural life will not flourish; for there is
a natural limit to the amount of goods that the husbandman
can produce. Consequently, he cannot attain to that opu-
lence which is the sign of God's favor.[20] But neither in the

---

[18]*De Reg. Princ.*, II, 3.

[19]Cf. Weber, Max, *The Protestant Ethic*, London: George Allen
and Unwin, 1930, p. 177; Fanfani, Amintore, *Catholicism, Protestantism and Capitalism*, New York: Sheed and Ward, 1939, pp. 208-9.

[20]The case is a little different with the large commercial farmer
who can hope for a large income through market crops.

teaching of St. Thomas nor in the common practice of his
times was this idea prevalent, i.e., it did not set the spirit
of the age. Though men were moved to amass earthly
goods inordinately, they did not do so with an easy con-
science. St. Thomas' teaching creates a different attitude
towards wealth: although temporal goods and the goods of
the body are good to a degree, yet they are all only secondary goods. This being true, it pertains to divine justice to
give spiritual good to the virtuous. In the matter of temporal good it pertains to divine justice to give the virtuous
only enough as suffices for the practice of virtue. It may
be that for some, temporal goods will lead to spiritual
harm.[21] Accordingly earthly riches could not be taken as a
certain mark of predestination. Here again Thomistic
teaching inclines men to be more satisfied with the moderate
amount of material goods attainable through husbandry.
Where our contemporary philosophy is alien to the rural
life, the Thomistic view was sympathetic.

The correct philosophy of life in regard to husbandry
and trading does not alone suffice to keep intact the hierarchy of values by which men live. Material goods will
tend to dominate man's activity unless the correct philosophy of life is given concrete expression through the practice
of sound institutions.[22] In this connection it may fairly
be pointed out that the student of St. Thomas' economic
philosophy would find his task much simplified had the great
principles of this philosophy been expressly linked by St.
Thomas with the institutions of his day, such as the manor

---

[21] Cf. *S.T.*, Ia-IIae, q. 87, art. 7, ad 2: Bona temporalia et corporalia sunt quidem aliqua bona hominis, sed parva; bona vero
spiritualia sunt magna hominis bona. Pertinet igitur ad divinam justitiam ut virtuosis det spiritualia bona, et de temporalibus bonis vel
malis tantum det eis, quantum sufficit ad virtutem....Aliis vero hoc
ipsum quod temporalia dantur, in malum spiritualium cedit.

[22] Cf. Tawney, R. H., *The Acquisitive Society*, N. Y.: Harcourt,
Brace, 1920, p. 180, who believes that today we must create an environment where greed will not be encouraged.

and the guild. The fact is, however, that no mention of these institutions has been found. It will be shown later[23] that St. Thomas' philosophy presupposes the requisite institutions, namely, a strong family, as the embodiment of the domestic order, and the manor and the guilds, as the embodiment of the functional order. His theory on wealth-getting in its relation to the family, and his teaching on the dangers of trade are to be found mainly in his commentary on the first book of Aristotle's *Politics*,[24] and are in part repeated in the *Summa Theologica*[25] and in the *De Regimine Principum*.[26] The domestic order and the science by which it is maintained *(oeconomica)* are treated in the *Summa Theologica* under the virtue of prudence.[27] The commentary on the *Ethics* of Aristotle also treats of these questions.[28]

Oeconomica, or household management, exists to regulate the affairs of the family in an orderly manner. This science stands in between *politica*, the management of the affairs of the state, and *monastica*, the management of a man's affairs in so far as he is merely an isolated individual. Closely associated with *oeconomica* is the natural wealth-getting of the husbandman which, according to St. Thomas, belongs to household management.[29] Because the family is left with natural functions to perform it is a strong institution. The family, as it finds a place in the Thomistic syn-

---

[23]Cf. *below*, chap. IV.

[24]Chapters 8, 9, and 13.

[25]Cf. *S.T.*, IIa-IIae, q. 77, art. 4; Ia-IIae, q. 20, art. 4.

[26]Cf. *De Reg. Princ.*, II, 3.

[27]Cf. *S.T.*, IIa-IIae, q. 47, art. 11; q. 50, art. 3.

[28]Cf. *In Ethic.*, I, 1.

[29]*In Polit.*, I, 8: alia autem pecuniativa est oeconomica, quae scilicet acquiret pecunias ex rebus naturalibus, puta ex fructibus et animalibus.

thesis, is a true cell of society,[30] a true regulator of production and consumption.[31]

The manorial group provided a further check upon man's quest for external goods. In St. Thomas' time it existed as a true functional group. Its member families cooperated in the production and processing of natural wealth, as also in the practice of the basic trades; for example, grazing land and equipment were used in common.[32] By reason of this functional organization a greater abundance and variety of goods was made available to the members of the manor. Yet such was the organization of the manor that this more extensive production and traffic in goods did not easily become inordinate. The production on the manor was directed to the needs of a particular manorial group, united by reason of community of place and function. For this reason it was naturally regulated by a limited end. St. Thomas approved the functional organization of the manor. It is in accord with his concept of the functional organization of society, and what is of present concern, such an organization helped to maintain a true scale of values.

2. RELATIVE SELF-SUFFICIENCY OF THE VARIOUS SOCIAL GROUPS

If man were an isolated individual, then the problems arising from his needs for material goods would be much simplified. He could go about procuring them, and using them as one who had no obligations to the common good. He would be constrained only by the rule of reason and that

---

[30]Cf. *S.T.*, Ia-IIae, q. 104, art. 4, c; *In Polit.*, I, 2; *S.T.*, Ia-IIae, q. 90, art. 3, ad 3; IIa-IIae, q. 50, art. 3. Cf. also, Ostheimer, Anthony L., *The Family, A Thomistic Study in Social Philosophy*, Washington: The Catholic University of America Press, 1939, chap. V.

[31]Cf. *In Polit.*, I, 8; *S.T.*, Ia-IIae, q. 20, art. 4, c.

[32]Cf. chap. II, 2, g, for the nature of this cooperation and to what degree it was free.

of the divine law. St. Thomas, following the Aristotelian tradition, insists that man is more than a solitary animal; man is naturally a political and social animal. If man were a solitary animal he would come only under a twofold order: that of reason and that of the divine law. But because he is a social and political animal he comes under a third order, that by which he is ordered to other men, with whom he ought to live in society[33]—unless he be a beast or a god.[34]

This third order has a great bearing upon the conduct of man. Not only in the spiritual realm, where it affects him in such activities as the search for truth, but also in the physical realm it will affect him in the procuring and consumption of material goods. By reason of this truth men are naturally inclined to cooperate politically to form and maintain the state. But this is not the limit of their cooperation. They must cooperate as a family group, as a village group, as a city group, and finally as a provincial group, if they are to attain the good life in full measure.

> Now, since men must live in a group, because they are not sufficient unto themselves to procure the necessities of life were they to remain solitary, it follows that a society will be the more perfect the more it is sufficient unto itself to procure the necessities of life. There is, indeed, to some extent sufficiency for life in one family of one household, namely in so far as pertains to the natural acts of nourishment and the begetting of offspring and other things of this kind; it exists, furthermore, in one village with regard to those things which belong to one trade; but it exists in a city, which is a perfect community, with regard to all the necessities of life; but still more in a province because of the need of fighting together and of mutual help against enemies.[35]

---

[33]Cf. *S.T.*, Ia-IIae, q. 72, art. 4; and q. 94, art. 2.

[34]Cf. Aristotle, *Polit.*, Bk. I, chap. 2, 1253a, 29-30.

[35]*De Reg. Princ.*, I, 1: Cum autem homini competat in multitudine vivere, quia sibi non sufficit ad necessaria vitae, si solitarius maneat, oportet quod tanto sit perfectior multitudinis societas, quanto

In the foregoing passage there is the suggestion that nature sets certain limits to the self-sufficiency of any group. Thus, it does not belong to the village, as such, to attend to man's need for nourishment; this is a family function. On the other hand, it does not belong to the family to carry on a trade. This is a village function, in which more than one family will participate. And so with the other groups. Elsewhere Aquinas teaches that the city group should seek to attain the highest self-sufficiency that nature allows. The city should not rely upon those outside her circle for those things that she can procure by her own activity; for, says St. Thomas, self-sufficiency is a mark of perfection in a thing.

> For the higher a thing is the more self-sufficient it is; since whatever needs another's help is by that fact proven inferior. But that city is more fully self-sufficient which the surrounding country supplies with all its vital needs, than is another which must obtain these supplies by trade. A city which has an abundance of food from its own territory is more dignified than one which is provisioned by merchants.[36]

The rule of self-sufficiency is a rule of good order; for it pertains to good order that any social group should carry on

magis per se sufficiens erit ad necessaria vitae. Habetur siquidem aliqua vitae sufficientia, in una familia domus unius, quantum scilicet ad naturales actus nutritionis, et prolis generandae, et aliorum hujusmodi; in uno autem vico, quantum ad ea quae ad unum artificium pertinent; in civitate vero, quae est perfecta communitas, quantum ad omnia necessaria vitae; sed adhuc magis in provincia una propter necessitatem compugnationis et mutui auxilii contra hostes.

[36]*De Reg. Princ.*, II, 3: Tanto enim aliquid dignius est, quanto per se sufficientius invenitur, quia quod alio indiget, deficiens esse monstratur. Sufficientiam autem plenius possidet civitas, cui circumjacens regio sufficiens est ad necessaria vitae, quam illa quae indiget ab aliis per mercationem accipere. Dignior enim est civitas si abundantiam rerum habeat ex territorio proprio, quam si per mercatores abundet.

all those functions for which nature has prepared it. It is part of good order that the smaller group should not be weakened by having its natural functions removed, and that the larger group should not be over-burdened by its taking over functions not proper to its wider and higher level of common enterprise.

3. Hierarchical Organization of Rural Society

According to St. Thomas this cooperation of men as social beings is not carried on in strict equality, i.e., men do not cooperate on one horizontal plane to achieve a common good. His teaching on this question is clear. Nature does not incline men to cooperate on one horizontal level; rather it inclines them to cooperate on many diverse functional levels to form an ordered hierarchy. Men are not equal in all things, though they do possess in common a rational nature, a common origin, and destiny. They differ accidentally in power of intellect, will, and of body.[37] Consequently, they naturally differ in their contribution to and participation in the benefits of the common good. These differences among men, St. Thomas regards as one of the necessary conditions of true order within any social or economic group having autonomous existence within the state.[38] Thus the functional and hierarchial organization of the manor is according to man's nature. It provided for the opportunity of socio-economic cooperation on a local basis, and it provided for individual differences. As a consequence of this fact of individual differences in men, there will be classes in society. But it need not be that the membership within these classes should be static. Thomistic

---

[37]Cf. *S.T.*, Ia, q. 96, art. 3, c.
[38]Cf. *S.T.*, Ia, q. 96, art. 3: ordo autem maxime videtur in disparitate consistere. Also, *S.T.*, q. 96, art. 3, ad 3, where he writes that God caused disparity, "ut pulchritudo ordinis magis in hominibus reluceret."

philosophy with much reason insists that the classes which naturally form in society be subordinated one to another, in a true inner unity within a hierarchy. The absence of this ordering is a cause of many contemporary socio-economic evils.

4. PROPERTY IN LAND

Where the fact of man's social nature was affirmed as a living truth, as it was in the philosophy of Aquinas, the question of property in land was approached with a clearer realization that the land exists for all men. This is not to imply that Aquinas favors a socialization of property in land. His teaching represents a *via media* position. Against those who affirm that property in land should be held by the state St. Thomas asserts that private property is according to the natural law;[39] on the other hand, against those who like the disciples of Locke in a later age, raise the right of private property to an absolute right subject to no limitations,[40] Aquinas teaches that private property may not be separated from the social trust or moral stewardship which are bound up in the divine plan with it.[41] This teaching on land ownership will later be studied in its relation to the feudal organization of 13th century Europe. Under the feudal system the land was spoken of as held rather than owned: it was held by the king, under God; by the lord under the king; and by the peasant under the lord.[42] Not all the aspects of this much criticized and sometimes

[39]Cf. McDonald, William J., *The Social Value of Property According to Saint Thomas Aquinas*, Washington, D. C.: The Catholic University of America Press, 1939, pp. 90-6.

[40]Cf. Larkin, Pascal, *Property in the Eighteenth Century, with special reference to England and Locke*, Cork: Cork University Press, 1930, p. 79.

[41]Cf. McDonald, W. J., *op. cit.*, p. 95.

[42]Cf. Jarrett, Bede, O. P., *Social Theories of the Middle Ages*, Boston: Little Brown and Company, 1926, p. 131.

misunderstood organization of the manor can be defended. However, the criticism leveled at this organization cannot with equal justice be leveled at Aquinas' land policy. His policy is not so intimately bound up with the manor that it cannot be applied with advantage in a different social framework. In this connection, too, it should be remembered that St. Thomas emphasized a law-making power of custom that was able to mitigate the force of the agrarian legislation of his time. In the philosophy of Aquinas the observance of those long standing customs of the manor by which the services of the peasant are fixed and his right of tenure secured is made a matter of obligation.[43] Authoritative historians on the agrarian life of this time state that custom actually did have a strong effect in such matters as the protection of a peasant who could not pay rent on his land and in the determination of the amount of his services to the lord.[44]

5. THE DIGNITY OF AGRICULTURAL LABOR

Among some contemporary social thinkers there is observable an inclination to look toward a future age in which an ever-increasing percentage of the population will be spared from the necessity of securing a living from the soil. The underlying assumption appears to be that the work of the husbandman is wanting in dignity. Such a change in the occupation of people does not necessarily represent true progress; and, if the number of husbandmen is to decrease in order that the number of factory workers may increase, then the result is retrogression. The following judgement pronounced by Pius XI upon certain kinds of modern factory work reflects Aquinas' philosophy of labor:

And so bodily labor, which was decreed by Providence for the good of man's body and soul . . .

---

[43]Cf. *S.T.*, Ia-IIae, q. 97, art. 3, c.
[44]Cf. *below*, chap. II, 2.

has everywhere been changed into an instrument of strange perversion: for dead matter leaves the factory ennobled and transformed, where men are corrupted and degraded.[45]

It is understandable on Thomistic principles why men should suffer degradation through such types of factory labor; and on these same principles the work of the husbandman will be seen to be capable of perfecting man, and compatible with the good life. According to a Thomistic principle of metaphysics and psychology[46] when man acts, he acts as a person; such is the union of all his component parts and faculties under the rational soul. In all his acts, such as the act of one's hand in labor, the person acts; not merely the bodily member. Consequently, the manual labor of a man is more than the repeated physical movements of the members of his body. Manual labor is performed by the person who is endowed with intellect and will. Herein is its dignity. Granted a worthy end, it retains its dignity as long as it involves the functioning of the intellect and the will. It loses it when, like to the activity of the brute which is determined *ad unum*, it allows no opportunity for the intellect to point out possible variations in procedure or for the will to choose among these possibilities.[47] The work of the husbandman is dignified if judged by these standards. Moreover it is noble in its purpose, namely, to provide the necessities of life. St. Thomas calls the work of husbanding the fruits of nature "praiseworthy".[48] The husband-

---

[45]Pius XI, encyclical letter, *Quadragesimo Anno*, America Press Edition, p. 38.

[46]Cf. *S.T.*, IIa-IIae, q. 58, art. 2, c: Actiones sunt suppositorum et totorum non autem proprie loquendo, partium et formarum, seu potentiarum; non enim proprie dicitur quod manus percutiat, sed homo per manum.

[47]Cf. *In Sent.* III, d. 33, q. 1, art. 2, q. 1, ad 3: homo propter hoc quod habet rationem, quae collativa est se habet ad multas operationes ...et ideo dantur sibi manus.

[48]*In Polit.*, I, 8: Pecuniativa...quae acquirit pecunias ex rebus naturalibus...est necessaria ad vitam hominum, unde et laudatum.

man uses his rational faculties to direct the organic and non-organic forces of nature to the production of new things.[49]

In part because of the inherent dignity of the husbandman's work, and in part for other reasons, notably those connected with the problem of social order,[50] St. Thomas may be said to favor the life of the people living on the land. A greater measure of peace is possible where there is a lesser concentration of population.

> That state enjoys a greater measure of peace whose peoples are more sparsely assembled together and dwell in smaller proportion within the walls of the town. For where men are crowded together, it is an occasion of quarrels and all the elements for seditious plots are provided.[51]

When Aquinas' concept of socio-economic order will have been explained in a later chapter,[52] it will become more evident why he should be of this opinion on the merits of a rural people. A widespread diffusion of husbandry is highly important if sound socio-economic order is to be realized. It is important if the State is to enjoy internal peace, the fruit of good order.

It is interesting to compare the teaching of Aquinas on this point with the teaching of one of the Fathers of our country, Thomas Jefferson. According to one authority on Jefferson, the latter "held firmly to the belief . . . that agri-

---

[49]Cf. *Cont. Gent.*, III, 21.

[50]Cf. *below*, chap. IV.

[51]*De Reg. Princ.*, II, 3: Denique civitas illa solet esse magis pacifica, cuius populus rarius congregatur, minusque intra urbis moenia resident. Ex frequenti enim hominum concursu datur occasio litibus, et seditionibus materia ministratur. In St. Thomas' commentary on the sixth book of the *Politics*, chapter 3, a section of the commentary that is more commonly now rejected as spurious, an agricultural people are explicitly said to be the best people. The reasons assigned there for this opinion on the merits of an agricultural people are interesting and similar to those in *De Reg. Princ.*, II, 3.

[52]Cf. *below*, chap. IV.

culture develops and maintains in every man the qualities
most desirable in a democracy."[53]   In a letter to John Jay,
Jefferson himself writes as follows: "cultivators of the
earth are the most valuable citizens.   They are the most
vigorous, the most independent, the most virtuous, and they
are tied to their country, and wedded to its liberty and interests, by the most lasting bonds.   As long, therefore, as
they can find employment in this line, I would not convert
them into mariners, artisans or anything else."[54]

There is some evidence to show that this similarity in
thought between Aquinas and Thomas Jefferson is not entirely accidental.   The latter was a frequent correspondent
with Du Pont de Nemours, a leading member of the physiocrat school of economic thought.   One of the fundamental
tenets of this school was that of the primacy of the agrarian
way of life.   On the authority of Chinard, Jefferson was
much influenced by this group: "like the Physiocrats and
like most 'philosophes' of the eighteenth century Jefferson
held firmly to the belief that the true wealth of a nation
consists in the soil and the productions of the soil; that
agriculture develops and maintains in every man the qualities most desirable in a democracy."[55]   Moreover, Max
Beer, in a study of the Physiocrats, insists upon a causal
connection between Aquinas and the French Physiocrats.
He writes: "the Scholastic influence, particularly that of
Aquinas, on the leading physiocrats is striking, and its
recognition will assist us to solve the riddle of physio-

---

[53]*Correspondence of Jefferson and Du Pont de Nemours*, ed.
Chinard, G., Baltimore: Johns Hopkins Press, 1931, p. XLVI.

[54]*Op. cit.*, Letter of Jefferson to John Jay, August 23, 1785, p.
XLVI.   Cf. also, Abraham Lincoln, "Milwaukee Address on Agriculture" in *Washington, Jefferson, Lincoln and Agriculture*, Washington, D. C.: Government Printing Office, 1937, p. 87.

[55]*Op. cit.*, p. XLVI.

cracy."[56] Whether or not a causal connection existed, it is certainly true that the emphasis on agriculture found in the writings of Aquinas is found as a basic doctrine in the economic system advocated by the Physiocrats.

If man is to attain to the good life, he must realize in himself the values to which he is inclined as a rational creature. In seeking for them, he must never be forced by circumstances to sacrifice the higher for the lower. He will be far from attaining the good life if secondary values, such as the material, preoccupy him out of all proportion, or if they are purchased at the cost of sacrificing the higher. The agrarian philosophy of St. Thomas, by assigning man to natural institutions on the land, such as the family and the community, and by stabilizing these institutions through a regulation of property in land, gives him security in the attainment of material goods, provides a natural check upon his quest of these goods, and allows him to labor for them with no detriment to his dignity as a man. To the degree that it can control him in the quest of material goods it will free him for the attainment of the spiritual. This much has been suggested by the brief survey of St. Thomas' philosophy just given, and will become clearer in the fuller treatment of this philosophy in subsequent chapters.

---

[56]Beer, Max, *An Inquiry into Physiocracy,* London: George Allen and Unwin, 1939, p. 59.

CHAPTER II

THE PLACE OF AGRICULTURE IN THE LIFE OF WESTERN EUROPE DURING THE TIME OF ST. THOMAS AQUINAS

For the purposes of this study, an adequate view of rural life in the Western Europe of St. Thomas' time (1225-74) is obtained through an investigation of the seigniorial institution—or manorial, as it is called in England—which is the important juridical and economic unit of this period. This is not to overlook the existence of the remaining parts of the feudal system, nor of those few independent small land owners who cultivated the soil apart from any seigniorial institution. The seigniory was itself only a unit in a higher level of organization within the feudal system. Thus the lord of the seigniory might himself be a vassal of a higher authority, such as the king, to whom he paid homage and military service. Inasmuch then, as we can attain to a satisfactory view of 13th-century agricultural life by concentrating our efforts upon the seigniory in its economic and juridical aspects, a study of the larger units of the feudal system may be omitted.

The larger section of the population was engaged in agriculture and occupied, in one capacity or another, a place on the seigniory. Perhaps because of a failure to distinguish between periods in the development of this institution, the seigniory is sometimes given an inadequate and unfair presentation in some popular books on this subject. There is evident an inclination to think of this period in terms of a few catch phrases: 'the serf tied to the soil'; 'the serf, whose place is little above that of the live stock';

20

'the serf, whose dark, miserable lot, unchanged decade by decade, is alleviated only by escape to the towns'.   Authoritative works on this subject, such as one of the recently published volumes of the *Cambridge Economic History*,[1] cause one to question the accuracy of this dark picture of 13th-century agrarian life, and suggest that perhaps certain aspects of this life are worthy of study.   Moreover, the medieval period is often treated with too much uniformity, as if the serfs—the unfree villeins—were as numerous in St. Thomas' time as they were in the period from the 9th to the 12th centuries.   Finally, there is a failure to realize that the early centuries of the Middle Ages were confronted with the serious problem of legal slavery, and with other forms of unfreedom, carried over from the period of the Roman Empire, and towards the solution of which the seigniorial institution was directed.   The evil and injustice of the seigniorial system, part of which was carried over from an earlier period, should not blind us to its achievements.

For a thousand years the seigniory, as it is properly called when the reference is to Western continental Europe, was one of the dominant institutions of Western civilization.   Its influence upon the social and economic structure of the European countryside extended from the early Middle Ages until recent times.   It was overthrown by the French Revolution and came to an end in Central Europe only as a result of the democratic movement of 1848.[2]   During this long period it underwent many and often very profound trans-

---

[1]*Cambridge Economic History of Europe from the Decline of the Roman Empire*, edited by J. H. Clapham, Eileen Power, Vol. I, "Agrarian Life of the Middle Ages," Cambridge: At the University Press, 1941.

[2]Cf. Bloch, Marc, Professor at the Sorbonne, "The Rise of Dependent Cultivation and Seigniorial Institutions," in *Cambridge Economic History of Europe from the Decline of the Roman Empire*, Vol. I, chap. VI, pp. 255ff, *passim*.

formations. For example, in the later period from the close of the Middle Ages, services to the lord from the peasants gave way to a great extent to dues in money or in kind throughout Western Europe and Italy. These changes notwithstanding, certain fundamental features persisted, and these defined "a distinct type of social structure, which had great resisting force and by which through the centuries man's destiny has been so powerfully influenced that even today in every country on which it left its mark, the divisions of property, the distribution of rural dwellings, the countryman's habits of mind, can only be explained by reference to its ancient and, now abolished authority."[3]

The limitations of the historical section of this study will not permit of a complete examination of the seigniory with all its transformations from century to century and from region to region. It will be sufficient to study this institution in its prototypal form as it existed in the 9th and 10th centuries, and then to note the important transformations it had undergone during the period of the 11th, 12th and 13th centuries. This is the basis for the general division of the present chapter into a study of the seigniory of the earlier period, viz., of the 9th and 10th centuries, and into a study of the 13th-century seigniorial institution with which St. Thomas was acquainted. The seigniory which was prevalent north of the river Loire during the Carolingian period, the important aspects of which were common to the seigniories of most of Europe, and the essential features of which persisted from the earlier to the later period, will be taken as the prototype.[4] As far as is feasible the subject will be treated from the viewpoints of property in land, of classes in the rural society, and of the type of economy that prevailed during the period.

---

[3]Bloch, Marc, *op. cit.*, p. 226.
[4]Cf. Bloch, Marc, *op. cit.*, p. 228.

1. The Seigniory of the Earlier Period

a) *Property in Land*

The classical seigniory was composed of two essential elements—the lord's demesne and the peasant's dependent holdings. The typical seigniories

> were distinguished by the union, and that extreme-
> ly close, of a very great area cultivated directly by
> the lord—the demesne, or as it was usually called,
> the *mansus indominicatus*—with little dependent
> peasant holdings which, following a rather later
> usage, we shall call 'tenancies' (tenures).[5]

1) The Lord's Demesne

Of these two elements, the lord's demesne is the more easily understood because of its greater uniformity of structure.[6] This portion of the seigniory was managed through a group of buildings—dwellings, barns, sheds, workshops—sometimes fortified. These were known as the court or *curtis*. Around it lie gardens, ploughlands, vine-yards, meadows. As a rule the demesne *(Manse domanial)* also includes forest land, often very extensive, and grazing lands which are generally subject to the rights of user by the community, and are not, therefore, so completely at the lord's disposal as the other parts of the demesne. Some statistics are available regarding the comparative size of the lord's demesne—apart from the common land—and the total of the holdings comprised in the seigniory. Even when limited to its cultivated fields and meadows, the

---

[5]Bloch, Marc, *op. cit.*, p. 228.

[6]The demesne is not to be confused with the domain, the latter including not only the demesne but all the land over which a lord had authority.

demesne remains very great. Its area will regularly be one-third, one-half, or sometimes almost even the equivalent, of that of the similar lands held by the body of peasants.[7] On this same point figures are available for a certain group of twenty-two seigniories of Saint-Germain-des-Prés as they were constituted in the ninth century. The total demesne area of these twenty-two seigniories was 16,020 hectares,[8] while the total area of the holdings was 16,728 hectares. The same author who cites these figures states that the generally accepted figure for the ratio between the culti-vated lands of the demesne and those of the holdings on the great domains (seigniories) of what is now France between the eighth and tenth centuries is "between one-quarter and one-half."[9] Some seignories, such as that of a lay lord near the monastery of Saint Germain-des-Prés, were small, com-prising only 120 acres of arable and 48 acres of meadow land. On this seigniory made up of the lord's demesne and nine holdings, the former covered 34% of the arable and about 57% of the meadowland.[10]

Such being the distribution of land between the lord and the peasants, it was necessary that the lord should have a fund of labor available for the cultivation of his acres. In the period under consideration wage labor played no import-ant role. On the other hand, on most demesnes there still lived some slaves who, being fed by their master, worked always under his orders. But these were incapable of meeting the need of the lords for labor. This was fur-nished by the dependent cultivators of the holdings within the seigniory. The complete discussion of how this was effected, involving as it does, the problem of classes or ranks in the seigniorial institution, is taken up in the next section.

---

[7] Cf. Bloch, Marc, *op. cit.*, p. 228.

[8] A hectare is the equivalent of 2.471 acres.

[9] Ganshop, François Louis, "Medieval Agrarian Society in its Prime," *Cambridge Economic History of Europe from the Decline of the Roman Empire*, Vol. I, chap. VII, p. 293.

[10] Cf. Bloch, M., *op. cit.*, p. 232.

Here it is touched upon merely because of its connection with the problem of property in land. For the present it suffices to point out that the lord received labor service from the peasants who held land under him, and who, as dependent property holders, incurred various obligations, a principal one being that of labor service on the lord's fields. The greater part of the soil held in this manner from the lord was split up into units, called *manses*.

2) The Manse

A complete and certain interpretation of the *manse*, "the master-cell of the seigniorial organism,"[11] is not yet possible; however, some certain facts about it are available. The *manse* was a customary unit of tenure in the seigniorial group. All the family's claims to pasture, woodland and water are part of this standard unit.[12] The extent of this unit of tenure varied; it was a function of the productivity of the soil and of other factors as well. The average size of the *manse*, at least at the time when the seigniorial institution was at its prime, was from eleven to fifteen hectares.[13] Originally the rule had been one *manse* for one family. Thus St. Bede spoke of the *terra unius familiae*, not of the little matrimonial family of later ages, but of the patriarchial family of several generations and of several collateral households living around a common hearth.[14]

The *manses* were divided into well defined juridical classes: those called servile and those called free. Originally the servile *manse* had been the holding of a slave, who had been placed upon it by the master in order that he

---

[11]Bloch, M., *op. cit.*, p. 230.
[12]Cf. Koebner, Richard, "Settlement and Colonization of Europe," in *Cambridge Economic History of Europe from the Decline of the Roman Empire*, Vol. I, chap. I, p. 40.
[13]Cf. Ganshop, F., *op. cit.*, p. 301.
[14]Cf. Bloch, M., *op. cit.*, p. 268.

might produce his own sustenance. The land was in no sense the slave's: it was only a detached bit of his master's property, who could take it back at will. Actually, the arrangement tended to become hereditary.[15] The free *manse* had been the holding of a free man, who, to consider but one manner of his becoming a dependent cultivator, may have offered his land to a lord in return for protection, and received it back, after which he held it from the lord and cultivated it dependently. Most seigniories, especially the greater ones, contained both types of the *manse*. The total number of servile *manses* estimated for Western and Central Europe were certainly much fewer, even in the period under consideration, than the number of free *manses*.[16] These two types differed in other respects. The servile *manses* are regularly smaller than those that are free on the same seigniory; also they have different burdens, heavier and—when services—more indefinite. More subject to the master's arbitrary power, they recall the lowly status of slavery.[17]

The nature of the *manse* is seen in a clearer light when it is contrasted with other types of dependent holdings, that might exist along side of it even on the same seigniory. Such was the *hôtise* in Gaul. Firstly, these two types of holdings differed in regard to the renders in money, or kind, or services due from them: in the case of the *hôtise* the liabilities varied; in the case of the *manse*, depending upon whether it was servile or free, the obligations were in theory uniform throughout the same seigniory. The obligations of a *hôtise* were the result of the circumstances of each individual case; the obligations for a *manse* were a matter of group-custom, a fact which illustrates the security enjoyed by those who lived upon this typical holding. The *hôtises* were considerably smaller than the *manses*.

---

[15]Cf. Bloch, M., *op. cit.*, p. 241.
[16]Cf. Bloch, M., *op. cit.*, p. 230.
[17]Cf. *Ibid.*

They were inhabited often by newcomers *(advenae)* to the seigniory. The man who had a *manse* had a real house, he who held a *hôtise* seems to have had nothing but such a hovel as the custom of many villages allowed paupers and immigrants to build for themselves on the fringes of the commons. Some surveys of Carolingian times suggest that the holders of *manses* were the only people who had a full share in the rights of the common land. It sometimes happened that the *hôtise,* through the addition of newly cultivated land, was later assimilated into the seigniory as a *manse* or a half *manse.* There were far fewer *hôtises* than *manses.* But a still more important feature differentiated the *manse* from the *hôtise:* its permanence. Even though two or more tenant householders might live on the same *manse,* this piece of land still remained a fiscal and administrative unit. In those instances where the *manse* was shared by more than one family the burdens were owed by the partners in common.[18]

b) Rural Classes

Closely associated with the problem of ownership of land as it was regulated in the seigniorial institution is that of the rural classes. It is possible to place most of the agrarian population—the nobility not included—into one of three general classes: at the bottom, the household slaves; above these, the servile villein; the highest in the order of dependent classes, the free villein. Between the members of these classes there is a rather clear-cut distinction based on tenure. Other agrarian groups, such as the *coloni,* the *colliberti,* the borderers, the crafters, and the cotters, existing at this time are less important since they can, for the most part, be reduced to the three classes mentioned above. Thus the *coloni,* originally independent cultivators, were in

---

[18]Cf. Bloch, M., *op. cit.,* pp. 265-7, *passim.*

this period villeins, some servile, some free.[19] The *colliberti* formed a group falling between the servile and the free villeins.[20] The borderers had small holdings bordering on open fields. These were migrants.[21] The crafters were hired hands and had no tenure whatsoever.[22] The cotters were very poor and held very little land.[23]

By the slave class of the 9th-century Europe is to be understood the class of those who were rightless men, i.e., of those who are of another—*alterius*.[24] The condition of the slaves fed in the master's house, called his *provendiers*, because they got their *provende* from him, approximated that of the classical slave. These worked as domestics, or as agricultural gangs working on the lord's demesne. The position of the slave of this class was a hard one: he had no civil personality and no legal family; he was master neither of his wife, nor of his children, nor of his possessions; he was almost in a class with the beasts.[25] However, this class, for reasons to be given presently, was a declining class and not predominant even in the earlier period of seigniorial institution.

By reason of the transformation, effected in large measure by the seigniorial institution, the slave class became what is known as the servile villein class.

---

[19]Cf. Boissonnade, P., *Life and Work in Medieval Europe*, London: Kegan Paul, 1927, p. 44.

[20]Cf. Boissonnade, P., *op. cit.*, p. 137.

[21]Cf. Thompson, James Westfall, *An Economic and Social History of the Middle Ages* (300-1300), New York: The Century Company, 1928, pp. 748-9.

[22]Cf. *Ibid.*

[23]Cf. Boissonnade, P., *op. cit.*, p. 92.

[24]Cf. Aristotle, *Politics*, in the "Basic Works of Aristotle", McKeon ed., New York: Random House, 1941, Bk. I, chap. 4, 1254a, 15: "He who is by nature not his own but another man's, is by nature a slave."

Bede Jarrett, *Social Theories of the Middle Ages*, Westminster, Maryland: Newman Book Shop, 1942, p. 103.

[25]Cf. Boissonnade, P., *op. cit.*, pp. 93-4.

The institution *(seigneurie)* itself, its fundamental principles, assumed a society in which
really servile labour played only an unimportant
part... Itself the antithesis of a slave system, the
seigneurie had grown up precisely when such a
system was on the decline. On this falling curve
of slavery the ninth century marks only a point,
but a point in fact very near the end.[26]

A similar analysis is offered by Thompson: "the practices
of manorial economy were repugnant to the perpetuation of
slavery in Europe."[27] This is likewise the opinion of
Boissonnade who states that the greater number of slaves
became, during this period, cultivators or agricultural
laborers scattered on holdings on the great domains.[28]

The existence of the servile *manse*, is of itself an indication of the declining character of the institution of classical slavery. One author of the Cambridge Study, who
offers a lengthy explanation for the decline of slavery,
places much emphasis on the economic factor as a contributing cause to this decline. Slaves were becoming more
difficult to acquire. Moreover, the working of great estates—the old *latifundia*—was no longer considered possible or desirable. The grouping about of a central establishment of dependent holdings, saddled with dues and services, was preferred. On these holdings labor kept itself
by cultivating some land for itself, reproduced itself, and
supplied the labor needs of the lord for his demesne. The
troops of slaves who had once lived on the great estates,
gradually decreased in number because their masters were
always turning them into tenants, 'hutting' them as the
phrase had it; giving to each his own hut with the necessary
fields. The result was the servile *manse*. In some instances the slave put upon the land was freed at the same

---

[26]Bloch, M., *op. cit.*, p. 234.

[27]Thompson, J. W., *op. cit.*, p. 744.

[28]Cf. Boissonnade, P., *op. cit.*, p. 94.

time; the *manse* of such a one would be free.[29]

This new group, which grew up above slavery, has taken the name of servile villein class. Many are included in this category. In strict law these slaves placed upon the land retained their servile status. They remained subject to a master's arbitrary authority; were generally excluded from the courts of law. The land they possessed was in no sense their own. Their holdings had defined duties that were often heavy and lowly. Their poverty and hardships present a dark picture.[30] On the other hand, the serf could not be sold off the land; he enjoyed a family relation, and he had security and protection.[31] Through force of custom the serf's lot, though far from satisfactory was not as low as in strict law it might appear to be. The serf though not protected by custom to the degree enjoyed by the freeman did, nevertheless, benefit from it. Custom regulated his obligations, making them less arbitrary at the will of his master. Under existing law the slave on the land was in a class distinct from the freeman on the land. However, due in large part to the force of custom arising from a Christian philosophy of life, the servile villein class did not remain in its low status, as sharply separated from the free villeins:

> From the ninth and early tenth centuries the various grades of dependent cultivators are in the process of assimilation into a single class, although originally they and their holdings had been in classes far apart. . . Official terminology, legal rules, with their strict lawyerly style, maintain as best they can the line between the free and the

---

[29]Cf. Bloch, M., *op. cit.*, pp. 234-243, *passim.*

[30]Cf. Bede Jarrett, *op. cit.*, pp. 105-7.

[31]Cf. Thompson, J. W., *op. cit.*, p. 745; also Belloc, H., *The Restoration of Property*, N. Y.: Sheed and Ward, 1936, p. 104.

servile tenant. Habit and common speech had already nearly erased it.[32]

Like the servile villeins the free villeins were dependent cultivators, but unlike the former they were free men. Some of these were free through manumission. Slaves were sometimes freed at the same time that they were placed on the land. To this group of free villeins belonged also innumerable peasants, by ancestral status free, who through commendation became dependent upon some lord. In the later years of the Roman Empire many independent cultivators found themselves forced by circumstances to seek the protection of a strong man. Among the many kinds of agreements for protection, there was one by which the small cultivator transferred his land to his patron. He was not as a rule actually dispossessed. He gave it to get it back again; but henceforward as a *colonus*. Individual acts of submission were not the only sort. Whole rural communities sometimes accepted a protector. After the invasions this movement towards submission increased. It took place in Western Europe, and also in England, where many independent peasants came to the lord and submitted their land to him.[33]

The free villein enjoyed the benefit of contract, which the servile villein was denied. The former gave labor services, but to a fixed amount. Usually the free villeins cultivated their holdings on the strength of leases, the conditions of which differed greatly. Some granted the land for a term of years or for life; others were hereditary. Some conferred almost plenary possession upon the villein. Lastly, there were leases which associated the owner and the cultivator more intimately, assuring to the former, in-

---

[32]Bloch, M., *op. cit.*, p. 241; cf. also Tawney, R. H., *The Agrarian Problem in the Sixteenth Century*, N. Y.: Longmans, Green, 1912, p. 407.

[33]Cf. Bloch, M., *op. cit.*, pp. 252-60.

stead of a fixed rent *(cens)*, a varying share *(champart)* in the annual produce of the villein's cultivation.

These payments, such as the *cens* or the *champart,* were given by the peasants to their feudal superiors in lieu of the homage or guardservice that were in turn given by a vassal to his higher lord. Enjoying perpetual usufruct of the land, the free villeins had property in use, in default of full property rights. Generally speaking his property rights were quite satisfactory:

> Originally the villein held his land only by an inalienable life tenure, but contracts and customs soon transformed this peasant holding into a patrimonial possession like the fief. The villein was the true owner of the land, despite the services with which it was burdened. The majority of the free villeins of the West were able to hand on their holding to their children. . .by simply paying a succession due. . . The land of the free villein could also be alienated, on the payment of of other taxes.[34]

In other respects the status of the free villeins was not entirely favorable. The majority of them possessed neither the right to carry arms for their defense, nor, as a rule, the possibility of changing their domicile or their lord.

2. THE SEIGNIORIAL INSTITUTION OF ST. THOMAS' TIME

The essential feature of the ninth-century seigniory persisted into the 13th-century form of this institution, but with notable changes. Most significant among these changes were those in land tenure and in the distribution of the dependent ranks.

---

[34]Boissonnade, *op. cit.*, p. 134.

a) Disintegration of the Demesne and the Manse

By the 13th century the demesnes of many seigniories were in a state of disintegration, due to such factors as the usurpations of estate officials, who found ways of appropriating for themselves both a part of the revenues due to the lord from the tenants and a portion of the lands from the demesne farm. Another contributing factor was the decline of labor services, which in an earlier period were an important tenant obligation to the lord. These industrial and agricultural *corvées*, once heavy, were much reduced during the period under study. A constant action and reaction took place between the decline of the labor services and the disintegration of the demesne. Moreover, the passive resistance of the tenants to these labor services had a like effect. The breaking up of the *manse* led to complications over labor dues, making it difficult to fix responsibility, and to exact regular services. Finally, the commutation of labor services for rents in kind or in money induced the lords to give up cultivating their own estates.[35]

Along with the disintegration of the demesne there occurred a parallel disintegration of the *manse*. By the 13th century *half-manses* and *quarter-manses* were recognized units. In some places of Western and Central Europe the *manse* remained only as a unit of land measure, having ceased to be a unit of tenure, or a rent-collecting unit. This break-up of the *manse* was caused in part from the need to divide lands in inheritance transfers. In those places where there occurred this early break-up of the *manse*, a regrouping of holdings followed.[36]

b) Land Tenure

During his lifetime, St. Thomas, who traveled widely over Western Europe, was in a position to witness changes

---

[35]Cf. Ganshop, F., *op. cit.*, pp. 293-5.
[36]Cf. Ganshop, F., *op. cit.*, pp. 300-2.

in land tenure, changes that tended in the direction of more freedom for the villeins. In the words of Thompson: "By 1300 the serfs, or at least several millions of them, had ascended to freedom, or if they were still called serfs, it was a legal fiction."[37]   Grants of land to the tenant for a term of years began to replace the permanent holdings of the villeins. The practice grew of dividing demesne land into smaller holdings let out to farmers for a fixed period of time. This was the fixed-term lease which assumed two important forms: leases in return for a share of harvest *(champart)*, and leases for a fixed rent *(cens)*. In the former type of lease the share of the harvest amounted to one-third to one-quarter, but most frequently to one-half of the crop.[38]   Usually special provisions entered into the lease by which the lessor agreed to provide a part of live stock or equipment; or the lessee would promise to follow certain rules of cultivation. The lord was inclined to favor this type of lease, both because it allowed him to share in the increased productivity of the soil, and because it gave him greater freedom in the disposal of his lands, giving him the opportunity to select a farmer or a metayer for his personal qualifications.[39]   If this is correct, then it appears that the alleged condition of the villein in which he was tied to the soil, represented in some instances a valuable security to him.

c) *Serf's Tie to the Soil*

Actually the serf's tie to the glebe in the 13th century does not seem to have been the great oppresive force in his life that it was in the time of the later Roman Empire when this condition was forced upon him by the laws of the land. In the Empire of the 4th and 5th centuries the

---

[37]Thompson, J. W., *op. cit.*, p. 799.
[38]Cf. Ganshop, F., *op. cit.*, p. 307.
[39]Cf. Ganshop, F., *op. cit.*, pp. 308-9.

colonus, formerly a free cultivator of the soil for another, became a man who could not quit his land and whom no one could detach from it.   For the sake of stability in a weakening empire he was tied to the soil.   In respect to the peasant's tie to the soil the condition in 13th-century Europe, especially Italy, seems to have been quite different. In the desire of the French lord to convert customary tenure into temporary leases[40] there is indication that the tie to the soil, if odious to the peasant, could also be odious to the lord.   Conditions of 13th-century Italy reveal that the tie was not odious to the peasant; they reveal further that the peasant was free to leave his land:

> The peasant had no great objection to being obliged to stay on his land.   What he most valued was the heritable right to its use.   If he had wanted to leave it the owner would not have stood in his way; in fact the owner would probably have paid something to induce him to give it up.[41]

Moreover, in Italy where the lease *(livello)* tended to become hereditary, the lessor "had little enough chance" of recovering disposal of the land from the tenant.   Even when the lessee could not pay his rent, custom often allowed him a long period of grace.   The ultimate reason for this state of affairs lay in the fact that the rent contracts were favorable to the tenant, and not changeable at will by the lord.   Consequently, the right to lease became for the tenant a valuable property which he would not alienate without compensation.[42]   In such a society, where these conditions obtained and where custom safeguarded the tenant, it is misleading to speak of the serf's tie to the land, as if to suggest that an odium attached to this mode of

---

[40]Cf. *above,* chap. II, 2, under Land Tenure.

[41]Mickwith, Gunnar, *Cambridge Economic History of Europe from the Decline of the Roman Empire,* Vol. I, chap. VII, p. 328.

[42]Cf. Mickwith, G., *op. cit.,* p. 329.

tenure. In the case of Italy at least, it appears that the
tie was a protection to the peasant lest he fall into the
class of the landless day-laborers, who in Bologna were
called, significantly enough, the *malnutriti.*[43] Circumstances do not seem to have been quite as favorable in other
parts of Western Europe. Yet even here the peasants were
in some degree mobile: "Liberty of domicile was admitted,
and the lord could no longer bring back by force the peasant
who had left his estate, provided that the latter had given
him notice, ceded to him a part of his movable possessions,
and furnished him with a substitute, or paid a special tax."[44]

d) Leases of the Free Villein

Returning again to the subject of leases, it is interesting to note that this new type of fixed-term lease, which
points to our present rent-contract, was nevertheless looked
upon as conferring true property in use. In Burgundy and
Auvergne, for instance, until the 14th century, and later, a
lease of land was treated as if it were really a sale, though
of temporary effect. The lessee was looked upon to have a
real property-right in the land.[45] From this it appears that
the fixed-term lease is yet far removed from the modern
rent-contract. Despite the growth of the fixed-term leases
the customary tenure, as of earlier times, continued to exist
everywhere.

e) Decline of Labor Services

The decline of labor services, already mentioned as a
cause for the decline of the demesne, was extensive. The
peasant holdings of this time have a common characteristic:

---

[43]Cf. Mickwith, G., *op. cit.*, p. 328.
[44]Boissonnade, P., *op. cit.*, p. 248.
[45]Cf. Ganshop, F., *op. cit.*, p. 308.

"They paid dues in money or in kind, to which labour services had become purely accessory."[46] The figures given for this period of decline of the *corvées* are surprisingly low. Where three days a week of agricultural services had been given in the Carolingian period, now, after the decline, only a few days—two, three, six, ten, occasionally, but rarely more than ten—would be given for the entire year. Such are the figures given for the seigniorial villages around Paris.[47] In Beauvais, which was, however, exceptional, the peasants from whom the *corvée* could be exacted had to furnish only one day's labor and three days' ploughing each year.[48] Sometimes agricultural services disappeared altogether. As a general rule, certain kinds of labor services, such as fencing, mowing, and haymaking *corvées* of the meadows of the lord's demesne survived longer.[49] Consequent upon this decline, the holdings became, during the 12th and 13th centuries, far more independent and the peasant's lot was improved.[50]

f) General Condition of the Unfree and the Free Villein Classes

By reason of these changes of tenure within the seigniorial institution from the 9th to the 13th centuries, the rural classes enjoyed an "emancipation."[51] Slavery ceased to be an important institution.[52] The lot of the unfree villein, commonly called the serf, was not slavery. There is, on the contrary, much reason for calling him a tenant, for he had come to share many of the benefits of the free villein, who has by this time become a tenant, and

---

[46]Ganshop, F., *op. cit.*, p. 311.
[47]Cf. Ganshop, F., *op. cit.*, pp. 295-6.
[48]Cf. Boissonnade, *op. cit.*, p. 249.
[49]Cf. Ganshop, F., *op. cit.*, p. 296.
[50]Cf. Ganshop, F., *op. cit.*, p. 312.
[51]Cf. Boissonnade, *op. cit.*, chap. IX.
[52]Cf. *above*, chap. II, 1, B, on Rural Classes.

who possesses more security than his modern counterpart.[53] The following evaluation, supported by much evidence, regards the serf of the 12th and 13th centuries as a tenant:

> Among the members of the *seigneuries,* in the twelfth and thirteenth centuries, many are held to lack that legal quality called freedom. Yet neither the French or Italian *serfs,* not the German *Eigene,* nor the English bondmen are slaves. . . Not slaves in the legal sense. . . their relations with their lords are fixed by custom; they have their own possessions; and no one regards them as human beings devoid of rights. Still less slaves in the economic sense: they do not live on the demesne; they have their fields for which they pay their dues and services; in short they are tenants.[54]

That the unfree villein is lacking in freedom is granted. He is unfree in the sense that he is bound to a lord by a tie that is personal and hereditary, a tie which in some fashion attaches to his body from birth, and which is rather degrading. But by reason of his tenure of land, and his protection through custom, he is not unfree in the classical connotation of that word. Actually—if not legally—his tenure, as interpreted by custom, has given him a certain independence of the lord.

The free villein is free because he can choose his own lord—as a vassal does. He is only bound to his lord by holding some tenure, or living on some particular spot.[55] He has liberty of domicile.[56] This class sometimes called *censitaires,* or rent-paying tenants, possessed the majority of civil liberties, and most of the prerogatives of real

---

[53]Cf. Belloc, H., *The Restoration of Property,* N. Y.: Sheed and Ward, 1936, pp. 103-5.

[54]Bloch, M., *op. cit.,* p. 242; Cf. also, Thompson, J. W., *op. cit.,* p. 799.

[55]Cf. Bloch, M., *op. cit.,* p. 242.

[56]Cf. Boissonnade, *op. cit.,* p. 248.

property. The following essential rights of property belonged to them: that of succession, donation, sale, and
alienation; they could mortgage or bequeath their holdings.
They were secured against eviction, on the condition that
they regularly paid their rents, which had become invari-
able and strictly determined by individual or collective contracts.[57]   And what is of great importance, this class was
protected, both in drawing up and in fulfilling these contracts, by custom, which reminded the lord of the social responsibilities entailed in his holding of the land from the
king or from some other higher authority, and which insisted upon the general truth that property in land is for the
common good.

g) Cooperation in Husbandry

A social structure that, like the seigniory, was able to
retain its essential characteristics for a thousand years,
during which it exercised a predominant influence upon
the agrarian life of Europe, would seem to have possessed
a true natural unity that ordered its parts and kept them
intact.   It is unlikely that the seigniorial institution could
have persisted through the centuries had it been constituted
by a mere aggregation of men.   Relative to its unity certain questions suggest themselves.   Is it to be thought
that the unity claimed for the seigniory rested merely upon
the dependent members' need for protection?   Or was its
unity only a unity arbitrarily imposed by a strong authority
upon men who had given up much of their freedom?
These factors—the lower classes' need for protection and
the strong authority of the lord—undoubtedly effected a
certain unity in the seigniory.   But these were not the only
factors, and they probably were not the most important
ones.   The members of the seigniory were united in their
cooperation in husbandry; and this was a natural coopera-

---

[57]Cf. Boissonnade, *op. cit.,* p. 253.

tion, that might well have continued even though all degrees of unfreedom had ceased to exist.

Such was the joint use of common lands and resources everywhere associated with seigniorial husbandry. In England, to select but one country where this practice prevailed during the period when medieval agrarian life was at its prime,[58] great stretches of land not under cultivation were considered as common land. This waste land was an economic necessity in any medieval society.[59] It provided food for cattle and sheep. In some instances the waste land was intercommoned by several villages all of whom had rights in the bits of fen, marsh, woodland, or heath lying between them. The *lex et consuetudo marisci*, sometimes having the force of law, protected these rights. Of more interest was the common use of common land by the members of one village. Such was the use of the uncultivated land of a village and of the woodland that had been cleared (assarted) by their joint effort. Of great extent, too, was the commoning of villagers on the fallow and waste of the individual villages in which they lived. In England the village seems to have been the unit.[60] Elsewhere the seigniory was the unit. A late 11th-century account from Barcelona records a similar joint participation in the natural resources:

> 'Flowing water and springs, meadows, grazing grounds, forests . . . and rock', the Customs of Barcelona record, about 1070, 'belong to barons not

---

[58]Cf. Neilson, Nellie, *Cambridge Economic History of Europe from the Decline of the Roman Empire*, Vol. I, chap. VII, p. 456.

[59]Tawney, R. H., *op. cit.*, pp. 238-9, writes that "common and common rights, so far from being merely a luxury or a convenience, were really an integral and indispensable part of the system of agriculture, a linch pin, the removal of which brought the whole structure of village society tumbling down." Cf. also p. 244, on the cooperative use of the commons.

[60]Cf. Neilson, N., *op. cit.*, p. 458.

[61]Quoted by Bloch, M., *op. cit.*, p. 271.

to be held *en alleu'* (that is, in disregard of any
rights but their own) 'or as part of the demesne,
but in order that their people may enjoy them at
all times.'[61]

The three-course open-field system of husbandry requires but to be explained in order to understand the cooperation it necessitated. In this advanced system of
husbandry, the arable land was divided into three fields,
more or less equal in extent, of which in rotation two were
cultivated every year and a third fallow. Common pasture
was customary on the fallow field and on the cultivated
fields after the crops were removed. The open fields were
large and offered much opportunity for grazing, no one
being allowed to maintain any hedges around his own strips
of land.[62] This type of commoning is recorded in the ac-
counts of medieval French villages. In the ploughing rules
governing this system of agriculture there is to be found a
parallel to certain guild rules governing a craft.[63] The villagers held meetings to decide to what use the fields of the
village were to be given during the season ahead.[64]

The seigniorial institution lent itself to a common use
of machinery. Since not all peasants could own a plow, for
example, a common use of this piece of machinery as well as
of others served them very well.[65] In like manner, ovens,
mills, and breweries were used in common. Much of this
equipment, which made possible an improved agricultural
technique and a somewhat more comfortable standard of
living, would not have been available, unless the lord had

---

[62]Cf. Neilson, N., *op. cit.*, pp. 439-40; p. 458. Also Parain, Charles,
*Cambridge Economic History of Europe from the Decline of the
Roman Empire*, Vol. I, chap. III, p. 128.

[63]Cf. Bloch., *op. cit.*, p. 341.

[64]Cf. Nabholz, Hans, *Cambridge Economic History of Europe from
the Decline of the Roman Empire*, Vol. I, chap. VIII, pp. 559-60. Also
Tawney, R. H., *op. cit.*, p. 244.

[65]Cf. Parain, C., *op. cit.*, p. 138.

provided it for common use. This was an answer to the problem of limited capital.

On the seigniory there was possible a division of labor that gave leisure to the lords and his agents, both ecclesiastical and lay. Such leisure was necessary for the growth of an educated class which in turn promoted, in some degree, the theoretical advancement of agriculture. At this time the great contributions to the art of husbandry came from the Arabian authorities. The advancement of husbandry in a theoretical as well as in a practical way by the monks may be taken as an example of the results of this division of labor.[66] Again, a division of labor on the seigniory or in the manorial village, where the manor and the village were coterminous, allowed for the advancement of the crafts, which were practiced within these groups.

h) The Seigniory as a Political Unit

The seigniory was a political unit of the medieval state. The lord exercised a real jurisdiction, having at his disposal the sanctions necessary to maintain order on his domain: he had the right to judge, to command, to punish, in short, to exercise powers normally pertaining to public authority. These were taken on by himself in default of a strong central government. This is not to deny that the lord's subjects suffered from great abuse of his power, abuses which custom frequently did not remedy.[67] Custom did however insist upon the general responsibilities of the lord for the welfare of those who lived upon the land which he held in trust from the king. The lord's position entailed a responsibility beyond the mere working arrangements of a business enterprise.[68] He was a public servant and in this capacity had a right to some services and dues in lieu of taxes.

---

[66]Cf. Parain, C., *op. cit.*, p. 159-60.
[67]Cf. Ganshop, F., *op. cit.*, p. 316.
[68]Cf. Bloch, M., *op. cit.*, p. 225.

3. The Effect of the Growth of the Towns and a Money Economy on Agriculture

The rapid growth of towns, the increase of commerce and the more extensive use of money were trends already appearing in the 11th century. By the time of St. Thomas they were well advanced. As a result agriculture fell in some degree from its position of dominance over the social and economic life of the time. Now a new social group appears within the towns, whose occupation and whose interests are different, and whose status is fixed by wealth and no longer by land tenure. Already here is the beginning of the great emphasis upon money values that is to follow later, an emphasis that will gradually weaken the seigniorial institution. These changes notwithstanding, a natural, agrarian economy seems still to have prevailed.

A number of factors contributed to the growth of the towns. Important among these were the increase of population, the rise of commerce and industry, and the growth in importance of the money economy.[69] The early townspeople were the merchantmen and artisans of the Middle Ages, who remained a minority group in St. Thomas' time. Some figures are available for Italy. Most Italian towns had a population of about 10,000. For the kingdom of Naples and Sicily—St. Thomas' native country—the total population was 2,500,000 in the 13th century. Of this group about 115,000 were in the four principal cities of this kingdom; and even some of these were agriculturists. But it should be noted that Southern Italy was more rural than its northern part.[70] The new townspeople did not always enjoy a decent standard of living. Some of these suffered from problems of congestion, high rents, unsanitary living conditions, and insufficiency of food. "In a word," one

---

[69]Cf. Thompson, J. W., *op. cit.*, p. 766.
[70]Cf. Mickwith, Gunnar, *op. cit.*, pp. 325-6.

author writes, "the latter Middle Ages—from 1300 onward —created the problems of the proletariat."[71]

The growth of a money economy,[72] that both caused and accompanied the growth of the towns, had its repercussions within the agrarian life of the time. The lords suffered from this new power of money, that often led to the alienation of their property,[73] and to penury.[74] Money opened the way to prodigality, which in turn compelled lords to raise loans upon mortgages or land rents, and also to accept rent in money as due from the peasants.[75] The new bourgeois class was anxious to invest in land, which by 1300 had become a commercial asset, an object of purchase or sale.[76] Their intention was not to organize cultivation as the lords had done but to gain a new source of revenue.[77] Far-reaching measures were taken to open the land for sale. To attain to this end, in some instances serfs were freed:

'The feudal system with its serfs bound to the soil on an hereditary tenure was a hindrance to the free investment of land. . . The towns of central Italy initiated the freeing of serfs en masse, not in order to give the land to the peasants, but in order that the towns might be able to invest in land.'[78]

The substitution of money rents, fixed by customs, for labor services made it impossible for the lord to share in

---

[71]Thompson, J. W., *op. cit.,* p. 793.

[72]Cf. Nabholz, Hans, *Cambridge Economic History of Europe from the Decline of the Roman Empire,* p. 554: "Money economy only partially superceded the natural economy on the land."

[73]Cf. Boissonnade, *op. cit.,* p. 241.

[74]Cf. Thompson, J. W., *op. cit.,* p. 801.

[75]Cf. Boissonnade, *op. cit.,* p. 241.

[76]Cf. Thompson, J. W., *op. cit.,* p. 802.

[77]Cf. Ganshop, *op. cit.,* p. 290. Also Ashley, W. J., *The Economic Organization of England,* p. 65.

[78]Carlile, *History of Money,* p. 257, quoted by Thompson, *op. cit.,* p. 803.

the increased value given to agricultural produce by reason of the increasing needs of the town population. This system of money rents which gave to the lord a fixed income and a greater simplicity in his administration of the seigniory,[79] was not without its evil consequences. Ultimately it made him subject to the new power of money, over which he had little control, and through which he suffered many losses. Where the lord suffered losses through the effects of the new economy, the peasant temporarily gained. He was able to profit by the increased value of his products, by the greater efficiency of agricultural methods and, in the case of the unfree villein, by the new opportunity to buy his freedom and go to a town if he wished.

Among the causes that contributed to the growth of towns and the money economy, and which for this reason also affected rural life, mention must be made of the Crusades. It is difficult to estimate the rôle played by this widespread movement.[80] On the other hand it cannot be denied that the Crusades were instrumental, along with other forces, in effecting far-reaching changes in agrarian life. They did so by hastening the formation and growth of towns. In many instances the townspeople were enabled to buy independence of a feudal lord because he wished to go on a Crusade.[81] The Crusades occasioned a great expanse of commerce at the end of the 12th century,[82] and thus hastened the expansion of a money economy. Because of this new economy the position of the nobility who now had to compete with wealth existing apart from the land, and

---

[79]Cf. Ganshop, *op. cit.*, p. 312.

[80]Cf. Passant, E. J., "The Effects of the Crusades Upon Western Europe," *Cambridge Medieval History*, N. Y.: Macmillan, 1929, vol. 5, p. 327, suggests that the emancipation of towns from feudalism would likely have taken place even though there had been no Crusades. Cf. also, Thompson, J. W., *op. cit.*, p. 433, who quotes contrasting opinions relative to the influence exerted by the Crusades.

[81]Cf. Thompson, J. W., *op. cit.*, pp. 794. 431.

[82]Cf. Boissonnade, *op. cit.*, pp. 160-1.

who suffered economic distress with the increase in the cost
of living, as reckoned in money values, was weakened. The
Crusades fostered conditions favorable to the emancipation
of servile villeins, many of whom became free farmers or
artisans in towns.[83] Finally, the returning Crusaders
added to the mobility of rural labor.

a) The Town-Country Unit

The towns of the 13th-century Italy[84] aimed at a certain self-sufficiency in the matter of foodstuffs. A significant number of town ordinances point to a policy whereby
the townspeople could be supplied with foodstuffs by those
who raised agricultural products on the surrounding countryside and carried them to the town markets. Traders,
apparently, were not to interfere with the flow of goods
between the immediate surrounding fields and the town
markets. Without some such hypothesis it is difficult to
explain certain ordinances. Thus some ordinances contain
a rule that such and such foodstuffs may not be engrossed
within a given area, which implies that the country men of
that area will keep the market supplied. Fruit-sellers, for
example, at Viterbo may not buy within a 4-mile radius of
that city.[85] Traders are forbidden to act as middlemen in
those cases where producer and consumer can exchange
directly at the town market.

Townsmen, anxious to keep down the price of food in
their own town and to lessen the dangers of famine, sought
by means of certain ordinances to increase the production of
food upon the surrounding fields. Apparently they did not
wish to rely too much upon traders. Such were the ordinances of Padua, for example, which prescribe that one-

[83]Cf. Thompson, J. W., *op. cit.*, pp. 795-98.
[84]The condition obtaining here differed somewhat from that of
Central Europe. Cf. Mickwith, *op. cit.*, p. 343.
[85]Cf. Mickwith, Gunnar, *op. cit.*, p. 338.

twentieth part of every man's land shall be in vines; and the ordinances of Sambuca, in 1291, which insist that there must be a garden for every hearth.   In general the insistence is upon those cultures which required more labor, but yielded greater returns.   Attacking the same problem from another approach, certain ordinances forbade laborers to work for foreigners lest the town land be not properly cultivated.   In keeping with the rule of a garden for every hearth, many townsmen cultivated fields in the immediate suburban district.   These would mostly be not true peasants but craftsmen and others who got their food supplies in this way.   It is estimated that in Chieri, where the plots averaged about $9\frac{1}{2}$ acres, more than a thousand families, comprising more than half the population, could be supported by this medieval part-time farming.[86]   Such practices point to a close connection of town and country aiming at a maximum self-sufficiency for the town-country unit.

4. EVALUATION OF THE SEIGNIORIAL INSTITUTION

Whatever may have been the faults of the seigniorial institution it yet merits careful study because of its achievements.   The agricultural institutions of the latter Roman Empire, in those instances where they were based upon slavery, depended upon the human resources of subjected peoples.   They required a constant influx of these resources to continue their functioning, since slave labor was not successful in multiplying itself.   From this point of view alone the seigniory was a superior institution.   Even in its worst aspects it solved this problem of labor by hutting the slave on some land, by giving him family life, and at least a minimum of independence, which in the very nature of things grew, because it rested on the ownership of productive property—the soil.   It grew to a point in the

---

[86]Cf. Mickwith, G., *op. cit.*, pp. 339-43, *passim.*

13th century where tenantry largely replaced serfdom. The system, despite its tyranny and its frequent injustices to the dependent holders, seems, however, to have offered man much incentive towards material progress. The period during which the seigniory exerted a dominant influence, was a period of great expansion:

> Never had the material existence of peasants been so favourable, and to find such conditions again one must look onward to the middle of the nineteenth century. A multitude of new villages, townships, hamlets, homesteads, and farms sprang up, and a crowd of parishes. In France the number was unsurpassed for 500 years.[87]

Before its efforts the forest, heath, marsh and bog, even in the coastal districts, the sea itself, retreated.[88]

Not least among the achievements of the seigniorial institution is the security that it provided to the common man who had no organization or power with which to defend himself. If the money economy was able to dislodge the powerful lords from their land, then how much more easily would it have expelled a class of small, independent peasants from their lands, had their small plots of land been freely alienable. And in the case of the small peasants the hardships would have been all the greater. The seigniory achieved much when it guaranteed stability of tenure to so large a part of the population. Stability of tenure, cooperative husbandry, and general prosperity—all these socioeconomic goods were realized through the agrarian practices of the 13th century. These achievements are notable; and if it can be shown that they are not inextricably bound up with a condition of servility in the lower classes, then the agrarian practice that allowed of their realization warranted the study that was given to it. The seigniorial

[87]Boissonnade, *op. cit.*, p. 260.
[88]Cf. Ganshop, *op. cit.*, p. 282.

institution incorporated in itself certain philosophical principles. It is hoped that the further study of St. Thomas' philosophy, to be undertaken in subsequent chapters of this study, will lay bare these principles and provide the means by which to sort out the true from the false, and to bring the former to bear upon contemporary agrarian problems.

CHAPTER III

AGRICULTURE AND PERSONAL VALUES

The ultimate end of society is to bring men, through virtuous living in this mortal life, to final beatitude after death, in the enjoyment of God.[1] That man may lead a virtuous life it is necessary that his living environment be conducive to health and that his occupation be worthy of his dignity as a rational being.[2] In this present chapter we shall consider the importance of agriculture for the realization of these ends, reserving for the following chapter the importance of the rural life in the attainment of virtuous living through sound social organization.

1. The Importance of Good Living Conditions

After a reading of the *De Regimine Principum* it becomes very evident that the Angelic Doctor has not confined himself to the higher reaches of metaphysics and theology but has also shown a practical interest in man's physical environment. Consistently with his belief that all that touches upon man's needs by that fact pertains to philosophy,[3] he has interested himself, as was pointed out briefly in a preceding chapter,[4] in all those details of city planning that are designed to further the good life. St. Thomas, in his letter to King Hugh of Cyrus, mentions two things that are necessary to achieve it:

---

[1]Cf. *De Reg. Princ.*: I, 14,: Non est ergo ultimus finis multitudinis congregatae vivere secundum virtutem, sed per virtuosam vitam pervenire ad fruitionem divinam.

[2]These two points are developed from Thomistic texts in sections one and two of the present chapter.

For an individual man to lead a good life two things are required. The first and most important is to act in a virtuous manner (for virtue is that by which one lives well) ; the second, which is secondary, and, as it were, instrumental, is a sufficiency of those bodily goods whose use is necessary for our act of virtue.[5]

The ideal city, he writes, should be located in a place where the air will always be wholesome. "The altitude of the place contributes to the wholesomeness of the atmosphere, because highlands are open to all the breezes, which purify the air."[6] The walls should be so erected as to give the people the maximum benefit of the sun. In order to guarantee a supply of food for the citizens of the city, care should be taken to select a place where agriculture can be carried out successfully.

Again, since to preserve health, a supply of suitable food is necessary, we must further judge of the salubrity of the place, which had been chosen as a town-site, by the nature of the crops indigenous to it.[7]

Moreover, nothing (except good air) so much helps to make a district healthy as pure water.[8] The inhabitants of a

---

[3]Cf. *In Polit.*, I, 9, princ.

[4]Chap. I, sect. 1.

[5]*De Reg. Princ.*, I, 15: Ad bonam autem unius hominis vitam duo requiruntur, unum principale, quod est operatio secundum virtutem. Virtus enim est qua bene vivitur, aliud vere secundarium et quasi instrumentale, scilicet corporalium bonorum sufficientia, quorum unus est necessarius ad actum virtutis.

[6]*De Reg. Princ.*, II, 2: Eminentia quidem loci solet aeris salubritatem conferre, quia locus eminens ventorum perflationibus patet, quibus redditur aer purus.

[7]*Ibid.*: Quia vero ad corporum sanitatem convenientium ciborum usus requiritur, in hoc conferre oportet de loci salubritate qui constituendae urbi eligitur, ut ex conditione ciborum discernatur qui nascuntur in terra.

[8]Cf. *Ibid.*

place must recommend it as a possible city-site by their good health, which may be judged by their ruddy complexion, their sturdy and well-shaped limbs, by the presence of many active children and of many old people.[9] That man may have the proper recreation, the city should delight its inhabitants by the natural beauty of its environment, to be enjoyed near at hand. For, as St. Thomas points out, "the life of man cannot endure without enjoyment. It contributes to this enjoyment if a place has a broad expanse of meadows, a heavy forest growth, mountains to be seen close at hand, pleasant groves, watered by streams."[10] The emphasis here is upon natural recreational facilities as opposed to contemporary emphasis upon the artificial.[11]

2. THE DIGNITY OF AGRICULTURAL LABOR

The dignity of agricultural labor may be judged in the light of St. Thomas' principles on manual labor in general.[12] The Angelic Doctor in his insistence upon the nobility of contemplation, did not lose sight of the dignity and value of manual labor. Every laborer may be viewed as an instrumental cause cooperating in the work of creation, extending it. By so doing he tends toward divine likeness.[13] Thus,

---

[9]Cf. *Ibid.*

[10]*De Reg. Princ.*, II, 4: Absque amoenitate vita hominis diu durare non possit. Ad hanc autem amoenitatem pertinet, quod sit locus camporum planitie distentus, arborum ferax, montium propinquitate conspicuus, nemoribus gratus et aquis irriguus.

[11]Cf. Ward, Leo R., "The Land and Human Values," *Catholic Rural Life Bulletin*, Vol. I, no. 2, Aug. 20, 1938, p. 3.

[12] Cf. Killeen, Sylvester, *The Philosophy of Labor According to Thomas Aquinas*, a doctoral dissertation, Washington, D. C.: Catholic University of America Press, 1939, chap. III, who has developed the Thomistic conception of the dignity of manual labor in general.

[13]Cf. *Cont. Gent.*, III, 21: Quum igitur per multa tendat res creata in divinam similitudinem, hoc ultimum ei restat, ut divinam similitudinem quaerat per hoc quod sit aliorum causa...Quod omnium divinius est Dei cooperatorem fieri.

by using his intellect and hands he changes trees into houses, marble into statues, and metals into machines.

a) *The Manner of the Husbandman's Cooperation with God*

The agricultural worker is distinguished from his fellow manual laborers in this, that it is given to him to participate in this cooperation with God in a unique way. Speaking of the destiny of man in the state of original justice, St. Thomas sets along side of the work that is uniquely God's the work that is left for man to do. As it belongs to God to keep man in the state of justice, so it belongs to man to make the earth fruitful.[14] This remains true of the husbandman's work today, whose responsibility it is to make the earth produce in abundance. For this reason high tribute has been paid to the husbandman's work by Pope Leo XIII:

> For that which is required for the preservation of life and for life's well-being is produced in great abundance by the earth, but not until man has brought it into cultivation and lavished upon it his care and skill. Now when man thus spends the industry of his mind and the strength of his body in procuring the fruits of nature, by that act he makes his own that portion of nature's field which he cultivates—that portion on which he leaves, as it were, the impress of his own personality.[15]

The non-agricultural worker, on the other hand, even though he does impart greater utility and beauty to the

---

[14]Cf. *In Sent.*, II, d. 17, q. 3, art. 2, ad 8: Sicut enim homo operatur terram ut faciat eam fructiferam, sic Deus operatus hominem ut justus sit.

[15]Leo XIII, encycl. letter, *Rerum Novarum*, May 15, 1891, in Husslein, Joseph, *Social Wellsprings*, Milwaukee: Bruce, 1940, p. 172.

things of the earth, yet he cannot really be said to be making the earth bring forth new basic materials. This is the grand task of the husbandman. When he acts as an instrumental cause in God's hands, he releases a host of natural, organic causes. He taps the fonts of productivity which God has placed in things. He releases for creative work the mighty potential organic powers of nature, awaiting actualization through him. This power has a unique excellence:

> The organic power is the free and distributed power. It is socially integrated power. It is resilient. It is repletive. It is under the law of increase through natural reproduction. It incorporates the amazing actuality of being mighty and at the same time of being delicate. Refinement of power par excellence it is—the mighty minutiae of the organic order.[16]

In the hands of the husbandman it can accomplish wonderful results. Wherever there is fertile land, sunshine, and rain he may plant a field of grain. Immediately a vast system of delicate machinery is working for man, gathering energy from earth and sun. This harnessing of natural energy for man's good is of a different order from that accomplished through the use of a fuel-consuming machine. In this latter case the energy released comes forth at the expense of limited natural resources, and the one who is using the machine is not rendering the earth fruitful in the creative way of the husbandman.

The husbandman's work of releasing and directing the latent energies of the organic world can be further likened to that of the teacher who, according to Aquinas, causes

---

[16]Boyle, George, *Democracy's Second Chance*, N. Y.: Sheed and Ward, 1941, p. 19.

knowledge in the learner, "by reducing him from potency to act."[17] Acting as an exterior principle, the teacher co-operates with an interior principle within the student, just as the art of medicine works with the natural forces within man and brings him health. "For in every man there is a certain principle of knowledge, namely the light of the active intellect, through which certain principles of all the sciences are naturally understood as soon as proposed to the intellect."[18] The work of the teacher is to cooperate with this active intellectual principle within man, in some manner to give it material to work upon, and to direct it in the work of learning. Knowledge is, accordingly, an effect which proceeds both from an interior principle in man and from an exterior one, the latter being the work of the teacher.[19] In this it is like to health which is likewise caused by both an interior principle—the curative powers of nature, and by an exterior principle—the art of medicine.[20] And as an effect, it is unlike to the form of a house that is caused by an exterior principle alone, namely the art of the carpenter.[21] The art of husbandry, which produces the fruits of the earth in cooperation with an interior principle of nature, namely, its organic powers, therefore shares in some way the dignity of the arts of teaching and medicine, and exceeds in dignity the art of carpentry.

---

[17]*S.T.*, Ia, q. 117, art. 1, c: Et ideo aliter dicendum est quod docens causat scientiam in addiscente, reducendo ipsum de potentia in actum.

[18]*Ibid.*: Inest enim unicuique homini quoddam principium scientiae, scilicet lumen intellectus agentis, per quod cognoscuntur statim a principio naturaliter quaedam universalia principia omnium scientiarum.

[19]Cf. *S. T.*, Ia, q. 117, art. 1, c: Scientia autem acquiritur in homine et ab interiori principio...et a principio exteriori.

[20]*Ibid.*: Sicut sanitas causatur in infirmo quandoque ab exteriori principio...quandoque autem ab interiori principio.

[21]Cf. *Ibid.*: sicut forma domus causatur in materia solum ab arte.

b) The Knowledge and Skill Required for this Cooperation

For this reason the art of husbandry requires a peculiar skill. Like the artisan, the husbandman must conform his activity to the laws of the matter with which he works. But where the non-agricultural worker need take into account only the laws governing the inert matter with which he works, e.g., the physical properties of various woods and metals, etc., the husbandman must conform to an order which includes much of the universe and is most intricate, for it is governed by the physical laws of living as well as of non-living things. He must reckon with the laws of the seasons, he must harness the mighty forces of the elements: sunlight, wind, rain, and cold, all these must be made to sustain life. St. Thomas was aware of this dependent cooperation. According to the science of his day he attaches much importance to the indirect influence of the celestial bodies upon the living things of earth.

> A consideration of the movement and location of the sun and the moon, and of the other stars is helpful in matters of agriculture and medicine. Their powers, their location and movement is better known to the angels by natural knowledge than to man.[22]

In this respect agriculture is given an honored place beside that of medicine. This lofty conception of the work of the man who husbands the things of creation demands that man make an endless study of nature's forces. He must observe and think.

It is in no way unfitting that an educated person should be engaged in this work, where he may use to particular

---

[22]*De. Pot.*, q. VI, art. III, c: In operibus agriculturae et medicinae, valet consideratio motus et situs sol et lunae, et aliorum stellarum, quarum virtutes, situs et motus multo certius cognoscunt angeli naturali cognitione quam homines.

advantage any knowledge he may have of such sciences as biology, botany, chemistry and physics. Confronted with the problem of combining labor and education in a satisfactory manner, Abraham Lincoln singles out agriculture as that human occupation which more than any other opens a "wide field for the profitable and agreeable combination of labor with cultivated thought."[23]   Moreover, the practice of this art offers the farmer a fine opportunity to develop the four intellectual virtues of wisdom, prudence, art, and science.[24]   Unlike the man in a city office, who may have ideas but cannot put them into practice physically, and the industrial worker, who may use his physical powers but on someone else's ideas, the farmer can have his own ideas and can carry them out physically for himself.[25]   The farmer is trained in resourcefulness, forethought and patience, all these things being the "necessary accompaniment of an agricultural life."[26]   In proportion to the measure of his knowledge and skill, he will be able to push back the frontiers separating barrenness and fertility, separating life and death.[27]

c) *Husbandman's Labor Is Worthy to Engage the Person*

In the introductory chapter[28] of this study it was pointed out that when man works manually, just as when he acts in any other manner, it is the person that works or

---

[23]Abraham Lincoln, *Milwaukee Address on Agriculture*, Sept. 30, 1859, quoted in, *Washington, Jefferson, Lincoln, and Agriculture*, Washington, D. C.: United States Department of Agriculture, 1937, p. 87.

[24]Cf. Hynes, Emerson, "Consider the Person," *Catholic Rural Life Bulletin*, 2:2, May 20, 1939, p. 11.

[25]Cf. Hocking, W. E., "A Philosophy of Life for the American Farmer," *1940 Yearbook of Agriculture*, Washington, D. C.: Government Printing Office, 1940, p. 1060.

[26]Penty, Arthur J., *Guilds, Trade and Agriculture*, London: George Allen and Unwin, 1921, p. 101.

[27]Cf. Hocking, op. cit., p. 1060.

acts. Therefore it is not said properly that the hand strikes but that man strikes with his hand.[29] His labor, even though it be physical, is nevertheless of a different order from the actions of brute animals blindly dictated by natural instict, and determined *ad unum.*[30] For man, who has the rational power of imagining various possibilities, and who has hands capable of a wide range of application,[31] various and diverse operations are possible.

Now, the husbandman is in a better position to work as a person than is, for example, the factory worker who must constantly repeat the same simple operation or limited number of operations, and who is in a sense determined *ad unum.* Under this aspect the latter has become dehumanized; and the more complex the machine, the more its operator is determined to one course of action, and the less human is his work. "The purely human, with its unpredictable possibilities, its curious vagaries, its moods and tempers, being nonrational, has no place in the pure rationality of factory organization."[32] The farmer, on the other hand, who uses simple tools, enjoys great latitude of operation in which he can take any of many courses of action that reason points out.

------

[28]Chap. I, sect. 5.

[29]Cf. *S.T.*, IIa-IIae, q. 58, art. 2, c: also *above*, chap. I, sect. 5, for quotation of the Thomistic text.

[30]Cf. *S.T.*, IIa-IIae, q. 47, art. 15, ad 3: In brutis animalibus sunt determinatae viae perveniendi ad finem; unde videmus quod omnia animalia ejusdem speciei similiter operantur. Sed hoc non potest esse in homine propter rationem ejus, quae cum sit cognoscitiva universalium, ad infinita singularia se extendit. Also, *above*, chap. I, sect. 5.

[31]Cf. *In Sent.* III, d. 33, q. I, art. 2, q. 1, ad 3. Also *above*, chap. I, sect. 5, for quotation of the Thomistic text.

[32]Briefs, Goetz A., *The Proletariat*, N. Y.: McGraw-Hill, 1937, p. 40.

d) It Fulfills the Purpose of Manual Labor

Scholastic philosophy gives first place in manual labor to that primary form of production, which is agriculture. St. Thomas assigned a higher place to agriculture than to industry and commerce.[33] Evaluated on the basis of the four ends assigned by St. Thomas to manual labor, agriculture merits a high place. Manual labor is directed first and principally to obtain food, secondly to remove idleness, thirdly to curb concupiscence, and fourthly to almsgiving.[34] Husbandmen furnish themselves and others with the prime necessities of life. For this reason their work has always been held in honor, and they themselves have the satisfaction of knowing that their work is not useless activity. The farmer, whose land is entrusted to him for the good of all, is a steward of the world's goods. In working his land he will more likely have a superfluity of goods with which to give alms than will the wage earner whose salary is always adjusted to the prevailing economy and leaves little margin for charity.

Agricultural labor, generally speaking, is of such a nature as to engage the whole man—his physical, intellectual and volitional capacities—and for this reason it tires the whole man. When the day is done the man is not divided: he is not tired in some one faculty or member and restless in the others that have all day been inhibited.[35] It has been said that the peasant "is filled with his occupation."[36] The

---

[33]Cf. Killeen, S., *op. cit.*, p. 62.

[34]*S.T.*, IIa-IIae, q. 187, art. 3: Labor manualis ad quatuor ordinatur. Primo quidem et principaliter ad victum quaerendum... Secundo ordinatur ad tollendum otium...Tertio ordinatur ad concupiscentiae refrenationem...Quarto autem ordinatur ad eleemosynas faciendas.

[35]Cf. Hocking, *op. cit.*, p. 1061, who speaks of "the all-round weariness that comes of farm labor."

[36]Belloc, Hilaire, *The Restoration of Property*, N. Y.: Sheed and Ward, 1936, p. 111.

constant growth of plants and animals engages his attention at all hours preventing monotony in the working and
home environment. The constantly changing rural sur-
roundings offer children opportunities for interesting play
as well as the occasion for the performance of many little
tasks. For these reasons agricultural labor is suitable for
keeping man from that state of idleness[37] which will harm
both himself and the community, and, by reason of the fact
that this form of labor absorbs man's physical energy and
requires his attention, it helps man keep in check his inordinate concupiscences. It helps him to bring his sensitive
appetites into harmony with reason. Much of our contemporary industrial and clerical labor is of such a nature that
it is doubtful whether it will bring these desirable results to
a satisfactory degree. In contrast to agricultural work,
factory and clerical labor in many cases engages only the
hands, leaving the mind idle. Moreover, these latter forms
of work are often repetitive and unpleasant.[38] In short,
this work is not an adequate challenge to the whole man.

Of its nature the rural environment is apt to stimulate
the unoccupied mind to meditative thought. Before the
eyes of the husbandman the secrets of nature unfold themselves, as do the thoughts of a book, revealing God in a
natural manner, and showing the dependence of all things
upon Him. To be aware of this dependence is to have
begun to be wise, and to have laid the basis for a religious
life. Apropos of this St. Thomas observes that in the
state of innocence agriculture would have been pleasant
from the thought of God's providence and from the consid-

---

[37]When St. Thomas assigns the removal of idleness as one of the
purposes for which labor is performed, he does not intend to eliminate
leisure or rest. These latter have their place and serve a good purpose both for the individual and the community. Cf. Killeen, *op. cit.*,
p. 76.

[38]Cf. Belloc, H., *op. cit.*, p. 111.

eration of the power of nature.[39] This remains true,
though to a lesser degree, in the present state. Today the
husbandman may see the plans of God for men, animals, and
plants constantly unfolding before the eyes. As Abraham
Lincoln noted, everything with which the farmer is confronted, from a blade of grass to the largest animal, is a
world of study within itself.[40] The one who husbands God's
living things will see his power manifested in the energy of
the sun, in the universal solvent powers of water, the car-
rier of foods, in the life of the soil, and in the organic life-
energy of myriad plants and organisms. Springtime, harvest, autumn—all these suggest corresponding spiritual
realities. St. Thomas was not unaware of this opportunity
for meditation in a laborer's life; while his hands are employed he can think of God and praise Him.[41]

Because man is a unity, his living environment and the
nature of his work will have a great bearing upon him in
the practice of virtue. If man's living environment is unhealthy, or if it is without the necessaries of life and without beauty or interest to him, then his life will be blighted
both physically and spiritually. The rural life provides
man with an environment and an occupation that are by
their nature suited to foster health of body and soul.
Accordingly, this life is conducive also to the practice of
virtue, granted of course that good religious and cultural
influences are brought to bear upon rural people. In all
this it is readily admitted that the explicit statements of St.
Thomas supporting this favorable evaluation of rural life
are few. They are sufficient, however, to indicate his
praise of the work of the husbandman. St. Thomas places
the husbandman's work in the same class with that of the

---

[39]Cf. *In Sent.*, II, d. 17, q. 3, art. 2, ad 7: In statu innocentiae non
fuisset agricultura laboriosa...sed delectabilis, ex consideratione divinae providentiae, et naturalis virtutis.

[40]Cf. Abraham Lincoln, *op. cit.*, p. 87.

[41]Cf. *Cont. Gent.*, III, 135: Manibus operando, possint de Deo
cogitare et eum laudare.

medical man. Both are arts; both require an intelligent and careful cooperation with the forces of nature, organic and inorganic. What is not had explicitly from St. Thomas can be arrived at by inference. Knowing his philosophy of labor and the ends he assigns to labor in general it is then easily shown that these ends are realized to a high degree in agriculture. In the present chapter attention has been confined to the values attainable in the rural life apart from any consideration of rural institutions. The importance of rural life in the attainment of virtuous living through sound social organization will now be taken up.

CHAPTER IV

THE THOMISTIC CONCEPT OF DOMESTIC AND OC-CUPATIONAL ORDER IN THE RURAL LIFE; ITS REALIZATION IN THE AGRARIAN PRACTICE OF ST. THOMAS' TIME

1. THE REQUIREMENTS OF TRUE SOCIAL ORDER

a) Its Constituents

Order may be defined as "an established succession of harmonious relations."[1] Its constituents, according to St. Thomas, are three: firstly, distinction with agreement; secondly, cooperation; thirdly, end. The distinction is necessary, for without it there could be no order. And if these things that are distinct from one another agree in no manner whatsoever, then they could not combine into one order.[2]

Before there can be order there must be a number of distinct things; in social order there must be a number of

---

[1]Marling, Joseph M., *The Order of Nature in the Philosophy of St. Thomas Aquinas*, Washington, D. C.: Catholic University of America Press, 1934, p. 28. M. De Wulf defines it as "La reduction à l'unité d'eléments multiples suivant un principe ou une raison commune," in "Les Exigences de L'Ordre Artistique", *Revue Néo-Scolastique*, Vol. XXI (1914), p. 261, quoted by Marling, *loc. cit.* Cf. also, Cox, John F., *A Thomistic Analysis of the Social Order*, Washington: The Catholic University of America Press, 1943, Chap. VIII, sect. 1.

[2]Cf. *In Div. Nom.*, IV, 1: Considerandum est autem quod ad ordinem tria concurrunt. Primo quidem distinctio cum convenientia; secundo, cooperatio; tertio, finis. Dico autem distinctionem cum convenientia, quia ubi non est distinctio, ordo locum non habet. Si autem quae distinguuntur in nullo convenirent, unius ordinis non essent.

distinct human individuals.   These individuals, with their faculties and appetencies, are the material cause into which the form of order is induced.[3]   Unless the form of order be induced into this multitude of distinct human individuals it will have no being whatsoever above that of the discrete existence of the distinct individuals.   For the order gives to the multitude its unity; and the unity gives being to it.[4] Consequently, unless the agrarian domestic group and the agrarian occupational group possess these elements of social order, then they have no claim to any existence or consideration whatsoever.   Moreover, if modern agrarian groups are to be patterned after their medieval counterparts, this must be done by reproducing in the modern groups those same elements of order that gave existence and solidarity to the medieval institutions.

Relation, along with the *ratio* upon which it is founded, is the formal cause of order.   "Relation is the unifying or binding factor that gives to distinct entities the characteristic of oneness.   It is in relation that order subsists."[5] The *ratio* will determine the manner in which persons will be arranged in a group, and the manner in which they will cooperate.   It causes the order to partake of a definite species.[6]   The *ratio* of the conjugal group, for example, is the complementary character of the male and the female; of the domestic group it is the need of children for care and the ability of the parents to give it; of the domestic group it is, in addition, the capacity of the paterfamilias for command-

---

[3]Cf. Smith, Ignatius, O. P., *Class Notes in Social Philosophy, 1941-2;* Catholic University of America, unpublished; also Marling, J., *op. cit.,* p. 33.

[4]Cf. Hart, Charles A., *Class Notes in Metaphysics, 1942-3,* Washington, D. C., Catholic University of America, unpublished.   Also, Cox, J. F., *op. cit.,* Chap. V, Sect. 1.

[5]Marling, J., *op. cit.,* p. 33.

[6]Cf. *In Sent.,* I, d. 20, q. 1, art. 3, quaestiuncula II, solutio I: Includit etiam tertio rationem ordinis, ex qua etiam ordo in speciem contrahitur.   Unde unus est ordo secundum locum, alius secundum dignitatem, alius secundum originem, et sic de aliis.

ing, of the servant to be commanded; of the occupational group, it is the ability in each member, possessed in unequal degrees, to produce some good or service. The *ratio* must be a common possession of each member of the arrangement. The *ratio* upon which the relations of the group are founded depends in turn upon the end or final cause that is desired.

When a desirable end is pursued by the members of a group, who will to cooperate in its attainment, or who are constrained by an authority to do so, then a social group comes into being. The end is the final cause of the social group formed, while the will to cooperate, or the authority directing cooperation, constitute its efficient cause. It is the final cause, or end, which is the most important determinant of the nature of a society: "In each case there is an end desired which dictates imperiously the foundation of the relations formed."[7] If the end desired is the procreation and education of children, then a group will be formed whose relations are founded upon the complementary character of the two sexes, and upon the dependent character of the offspring. St. Thomas shows how a diversity of ends, ranging from the satisfaction of man's basic needs, to the satisfaction of his needs for the full life, will give rise to various social groups within the state, whose organization is, in each case, proportioned to their respective ends:

> There is, indeed, to some extent sufficiency for life in one family of one household, namely in so far as pertains to the natural acts of nourishment and the begetting of offspring, and other things of this kind; it exists, furthermore, in one village with regard to those things which belong to one trade; but it exists in a city, which is a perfect community, with regard to all the necessities of life; but still more in a province because of the

---

[7]Marling, J., *op. cit.*, p. 37.

need of fighting together and of mutual help against enemies.[8]

b) The Element of Distinctio in Order

St. Thomas places great stress upon the individual differences among men. An enumeration of these differences, as St. Thomas has observed them, will bring out the meaning of his phrase stating, that where there is no distinction, there order can have no place.[9] Men form one hierarchy because they are all of one species.[10] But within this species there are pronounced accidental differences. Even in the state of innocence men would have been unequal in soul and in body.[11] In the soul there would have been differences relative to justice and knowledge.[12] St. Thomas recognizes that not all use their minds with the same diligence. Consequently, they will differ in knowledge.[13] In

---

[8]*De Reg. Princ.*, I, 1: Habetur siquidem aliqua vitae sufficientia in familia domus unius, quantum scilicet ad naturales actus nutritionis, et prolis generandae, et aliorum hujusmodi: in uno autem vico, quantum ad ea quae ad unum artificium pertinent; in civitate vero, quae est perfecta communitas, quantum ad omnia necessaria vitae: sed adhuc magis in provincia una propter necessitatem compugnationis, et mutui auxilii contra hostes. Phelan transl., pp. 38-9.

[9]Cf. *In Div. Nom.*, IV, 1: Ubi non est distinctio, ordo locum non habet.

[10]Cf. *In Sent.*, II, d. 9, q. 1, art. 3, ad 2m: Omnes homines sunt unius speciei; et ideo in omnibus est unus modus communis recipiendi divinas illuminationes, et propter hoc omnium est hierarchia una.

[11]Cf. *S.T.*, Ia, q. 96, art. 3, c: Necesse est in statu innocentiae aliquam disparitatem fuisse, saltem quoad sexum; potuit tamen in anima et corpore esse etiam aliqua inequalitas.

[12]Cf. *Ibid*: Necesse est dicere aliquam disparitatem in primo statu futuram fuisse...secundum animam diversitas fuisset et quantum ad justitiam, et quantum ad scientiam.

[13]Cf. *Ibid.*: Non enim ex necessitate homo operatur, sed per liberum arbitrium, ex quo homo habet quod possit magis et minus animam applicare ad aliquid faciendam, vel volendum, vel cognoscendum; unde quidem magis profecissent in justitia et scientia, quam alii.

body men will differ in strength, in size, in beauty, and in complexion.[14]   Accordingly, St. Thomas would place a distinction upon the proposition that all men are born equal: they are equal as sharing in one common specific nature and as created for one purpose; they are unequal in perfection of body and soul. It is because of this inequality that men lend themselves to the formation of ordered groups, such as the domestic group, or the political group, or the occupational group. These differences, far from representing defects in the plan of God or in the order of nature, are necessary that the beauty of order might shine forth from creation.

> The cause of inequality could be on the part of God. . . so that the beauty of order would the more, shine forth among men. Inequality might also arise on the part of nature as above described, without any defect of nature.[15]

Moreover, it would be unfitting that the superior person should not use his talents for the benefit of others.[16]

2. THE RURAL DOMESTIC GROUP

Both in the teaching of Aquinas as well as in the socio-economic practice of his time, the domestic group was

---

[14]Cf. *Ibid.:* Ex parte etiam corporis poterat esse disparitas. . .aliqui robustiores corpore generarentur quam alii, et majores, et pulchriores, et melius complexionati.

[15]S. *T.*, Ia, q. 96, art. 3, ad 3: Causa disparitatis poterat esse ex parte Dei. . .ut pulchritudo ordinis magis in hominibus reluceret. Et etiam ex parte naturae poterat disparitas causari secundum praedictum modum absque aliquo defectu naturae.

[16]Cf. *S.T.*, Ia, q. 96, art. 4, c: Si unus homo habuisset super alios supereminentiam scientiae et justitiae, inconveniens fuisset; nisi hoc exequeretur in utilitatem aliorum.

a primary institution, a true cell of society.[17]   So important is the domestic order, that St. Thomas numbers it in the fourfold order that is to be found in every people:

> Now in every people a fourfold order is to be found: one, of the people's sovereign to his subjects; a second, of the subjects among themselves; a third, of the citizens to foreigners; a fourth, of members of the same household.[18]

When St. Thomas writes of the domestic order, it is hardly conceivable that in his own mind he did not give a primary place to the rural domestic group. As a frequent traveller he was familiar with the various types of domestic society functioning in Western Europe. He was aware of the predominance of the rural domestic group. It is difficult to think that he did not place great value upon this group as a means by which to give men a sound socio-economic ordering, and through which they might find a stable place in society. For such was the population distribution of his time that the larger part of the domestic households were *de facto* living upon the land.[19]   And if the rural domestic group is analyzed, it will be found that in its singleness of purpose, in the close relation obtaining among its members, and in its cooperative functioning, it was a strongly united group.   It will be found that the rural domestic group of the Middle Ages possessed in a high de-

---

[17]Cf. *S.T.*, Ia-IIae, q. 104, art. 4, c; *In Polit.*, I, 2; *S.T.*, Ia-IIae, q. 90, art. 3, ad 3; IIa-IIae, q. 50, art. 3; also, Ostheimer, Anthony, L., *The Family, A Thomistic Study in Social Philosophy*, Washington: The Catholic University of America Press, 1939, chap. V. For historical background, Cf. *above*, chap. II.

[18]*S.T.*, Ia-IIae, q. 104, art. 4, c: quadruplex autem ordo in aliquo populo invenire potest: unus quidem principum populi ad subditos; alius autem subditorum ad invicem; tertius autem eorum qui sunt de populo, ad extraneos; quartus autem ad domesticos. Cf. also, q. 105, art. 4, on the domestic order.

[19]Cf. *above*, chap. II.

gree the three elements of true order, and made a very important contribution to the body politic, as St. Thomas conceived of it.

a) The Element of Distinctio within the Rural Domestic Group

The members of the rural household—the paterfamilias, who was husband, father, master; the wife, and the servants—were sufficiently distinct from one another to admit of a natural subordination among them. In the same household there exist "the order of the father to his son; of the wife to her husband; of the master to his servant."[20] The dominion of master over servant existed upon the seigniory according to various degrees. In some instances it was nothing other than slavery. This institution was fortunately on the decline in the agrarian life of St. Thomas' time, but not completely. St. Thomas discusses this problem; and his teachings on natural slavery have recently been made the subject of a doctoral dissertation.[21]

1) Servile Subjection in the Rural Domestic Group

St. Thomas observes a twofold subjection between men. The one is servile because it subjects one man to the good of another; the other is not, because it exists for the utility and good of the subjects themselves.

> Subjection is twofold. One is servile, by virtue of which a superior makes use of a subject for his own benefit. . . .There is another kind of subjection, which is called economic or civil, whereby

---

[20]*S.T.*, Ia-IIae, q. 104, art. 4, c: Patris ad filium, uxoris ad virum, et domini ad servum.

[21]Cf. Ashley, W. N., *Theory of Natural Slavery according to St. Thomas*, Notre Dame, Ind.: Notre Dame University, 1941.

the superior makes use of his subjects for their own benefit and good.[22]

The slave, in the Aristotelian sense of that word is under servile subjection. This is the subjection of one "who is by nature not his own but another man's."[23] St. Thomas did not accept slavery in the Aristotelian sense that the slave was *"alterius."* He insisted that slavery could not violate the basic rights of man.[24] He distinguished between a slavery of the body and of the soul. In those things which pertain to the interior movement of the will, one man is not held to obey another man, but God alone.[25] Yet a slave *(servus)* may be bound to obey a master in carrying out servile work.[26] The servitude by which man is subject to man pertains to the body, not to the soul.[27]

Servile subjection would not have existed in that state of human nature existing before moral disorder was introduced through sin.[28] It represents a type of dominion that would not have existed in a more ideal state of human nature, except over irrational creatures; for a rational creature, inasmuch as he is of himself, should not be ordered to

---

[22]*S.T.*, Ia, q. 92, art. 1, ad 2: Duplex est subjectio. Una servilis, secundum quam praesidens utitur subjecto ad sui ipsius utilitatem... Est autem alia subjectio oeconomica, vel civilis, secundum quam praesidens utitur subjectis ad eorum utilitatem et bonum. Cf. also, *In Sent.* II, d. 44, q. 1, art. 3, c.

[23]Aristotle, *Politics*, in McKeon edit., *Basic Works of Aristotle*, New York: Random House, 1941, Bk. I, Ch. 4, 1254a, 15.

[24]Cf. Ashley, W. N., *op. cit.*, conclusions of his study, pp. 140-146.

[25]Cf. *S.T.*, IIa-IIae, q. 104, art. 5, c: In his quae pertinent ad interiorem motum voluntatis, homo non tenetur homini obedire, sed solum Deo.

[26]Cf. *Ibid:* Servus domino in his quae pertinent ad servilia opera exequenda (tenetur obedire).

[27]Cf. *S.T.*, IIa-IIae, q. 104, art. 6, c: Servitus, qua homo homini subjicitur, ad corpus pertinet, non ad animam.

[28]Cf. *S.T.*, Ia, q. 92, art. 1, ad 2: Talis subjectio introducta est post peccatum.

serve as an end for another, as man to man.[29]   But if a man is subjected to another in this manner, it is because now, through sin, he may in some way be compared to irrational creatures; somewhat as Aristotle compares a slave to a mere instrument.[30]

The institution of servitude is based upon the *jus gentium* inasmuch as nations have found a certain utility following from this institution.   Absolutely speaking there is no reason why one should be a slave rather than another. Nevertheless, peoples have found it useful that the less wise man should be ruled by another wiser than himself; and that the one who can rule should be helped by the other. Here St. Thomas accepts the argument of Aristotle.[31]   St. Thomas merely tolerated this institution of slavery that derived from the law of the nations.[32]   Non-servile subjection, on the other hand, arising from the natural accidental inequality among men, was not incompatible with an ideal state of humanity and was favored by Aquinas without any qualifications.   The seigniorial practice of his day, in which classical slavery—servile subjection—was gradually giving way to peasantry, reflected his teaching.[33]   Even though the thirteenth-century villeins still lived in some degree of un-freedom, the tendency, nevertheless, was from servile to non-servile subjection.   A seigniorial institution, entirely free of servile subjection would have been in accord with Thomistic teaching.

2) Non-servile Subjection in the Rural Domestic Group

Along with the servile subjection among men that gives rise to slavery, St. Thomas recognizes, as was noted

---

[29]Cf. *In Sent.* II, d. 44, q. 1, art. 3, c: Sed creatura rationalis, quantum est de se, non ordinatur ut ad finem ad aliam, ut homo ad hominem.

[30]Cf. *Ibid.*: Sed si hoc fiat, non erit nisi inquantum homo propter peccatum irrationalibus creaturis comparatur; unde etiam Philosophus, ibidem, servum comparat organo.

above,[34] another form of subjection which is non-servile, because it exists for the utility and good of the subjects themselves. This is the form of subjection that exists within the household. Household or economic,[35] and civil, are the two divisions of this subjection recognized by St. Thomas:

> There is another kind of subjection, which is called economic or civil, whereby the superior makes use of his subjects for their own benefit and good.[36]

Subjection within the household would have existed even before sin entered into the world, which is to say, that this condition is compatible with a state of humanity unaffected by moral disorder. For, St. Thomas argues, if one part of the people were not ruled by those who are more wise, then, the multitude would be lacking in good order. "This kind of subjection existed even before sin. For good order would have been wanting in the human family if some were

---

[31]Cf. *S.T.*, IIa-IIae, q. 57, art. 3, ad 2: Quod hunc hominem esse servum, absolute considerando, magis quam alium, non habet rationem naturalem, sed solum secundum aliquam utilitatem consequentem, inquantum utile est huic quod regatur a sapientiori, et illi quod ab hoc juvetur, ut dicitur (*Polit.*, lib. 1, cap. 5, circ. fin.). Et ideo servitus pertinens ad jus gentium est naturalis secundo modo, sed non primo modo.

[32]Cf. McDonald, William J., *The Social Value of Property According to St. Thomas*, Washington, D. C.: Catholic University of America Press, 1939, on the *Jus Gentium*, pp. 81-96.

[33]Cf. *above*, chap. II.

[34]Cf. *above*, chap. IV.

[35]*Oeconomica*, a term taken from Aristotle and meaning the science of household management. *Politics*, Bk. I, chap. 3; *S.T.*, IIa-IIae, q. 47, art. 11; q. 50, art. 3.

[36]*S.T.*, Ia, q. 92, art. 1, ad 2: Est autem alia subjectio oeconomica, vel civilis, secundum quam praesidens utitur subjectis ad eorum utilitatem et bonum.

not governed by others wiser than themselves."[37]

It is essential to non-servile subjection that it should exist for the good of the subjects or the common good. "But a man is the master of a free subject, by directing him either towards his proper welfare, or to the common good."[38] In those instances of seigniorial practice where the lord, acting as the master, in the master-servant relationship, gave direction to dependent cultivators, i.e., to the free villeins in return for labor services and other dues, there was realized a subjection for the common good. This relation of the free villein to the lord of the seigniory is properly regarded as an adaptation or extension of the master-servant relationship which, in turn, is a part of the subjection within the household. It is not servile subjection, and in its economic aspects it is not civil subjection. As paterfamilias the lord provided a rule which redounded to the common good, and the free villein, on his part, fulfilled some of the functions of the servant.

It is more difficult to judge the case of the unfree villein in regard to his subjection under the lord. In those

---

[37]*S.T.*, Ia, q. 92, art. 1, ad 2: Ista subjectio fuisset etiam ante peccatum. Defuisset enim bonum ordinis in humana multitudine, si quidam per alios sapientiores gubernati non fuissent.

[38]*S.T.*, Ia, q. 96, art. 4, c: Tunc vero dominatur aliquis alteri ut libero, quando dirigit ipsum ad proprium bonum ejus qui dirigitur, vel ad bonum commune.

St. Augustine writes of this non-servile subjection within the domestic circle for the common good: "for this is the foundation of domestic peace, which is an orderly rule, and subjection in the parts of the family, wherein the provisors are the commanders, as husband over his wife; parents over their children, and masters over their servants: and they that are provided for, obey...the commanders are indeed the servants of those they seem to command: ruling not in ambition, but being bound by careful duty: not in proud sovereignty, but in nourishing pity. Thus has nature's order prescribed, and man by God was thus created." *City of God*, Bk. 19, ch. 14 in fin.—ch. 15, unabridged ed.; or, Bk. 15, ch. 14 in fin. ch. 15, in abridged Dent ed. London: Dent and Sons, 1931.

cases where he was under a despotic lord who selfishly exploited him, there he may be said to have been under servile subjection. But there were other cases in which custom had raised his position near to that of the free villein, and gave him certain benefits, such as of stable land tenure.[39] In these cases, even though his subjection remained servile before the law, it was a subjection that tended in the direction of non-servility by reason of the elements of freedom that came with stable tenure of land.[40]

The seigniorial institution was important because it allowed for an ample exercise of the economic rule, and because it reduced servile subjection and replaced it with a subjection, in some cases, entirely free; in others, with a subjection participating in at least some of the benefits of non-servile subjection. The master-servant relationship carried far less un-freedom in the seigniorial system than in the earlier *latifundia* which depended upon classical slavery.

It was pointed out that the seigniory was a political unit in the wider organization of the state.[41] The lord's authority extended beyond his own household and outside the sphere of the economic, over all those dependent cultivators over whom he had come to have certain powers, today reserved to the state or to some political unit within the state. St. Thomas would have favored such a rule of the lord, if it redounded to the common good. He would have favored the seigniory as an institution through which the wiser man could exercise an ordered rule over the seigniorial or the village group:

> If one man surpassed another in knowledge and virtue, this would not have been fitting unless

[39]Cf. *above*, chap. II, sect. 2, B.

[40]St. Thomas nowhere speaks of a subjection falling in between servile and non-servile. Cf. *S.T.*, IIa-IIae, q. 183, art. 1, c and ad 3; Ia, q. 92, art. 1, ad 2.

[41]Cf. *above*, chap. II, sect. 2.

these gifts conduced to the benefit of others.[42]

On the assumption that one man has a superior knowledge of the order of reason to which all men alike are subject,[43] and on the additional assumption that he directs others justly according to this order of reason, as he has the light to know it, then, he necessarily directs them to their own good. This principle applies not only to the rule of the lord over the seigniory but to all political rule.

In this teaching St. Thomas shows the influence of St. Augustine, whom he quotes in his article on the subjection of man to man.

> If one man surpassed another in knowledge . . . . Wherefore Augustine says *(De Civ. Dei* xix, 14)*:* 'Just men command not by the love of domineering, but by the service of counsel:' and *(ibid.,* 'The natural order of things requires this; and thus did God make man.'[44]

This passage from the 14th and 15th chapters of St. Augustine's *City of God*, cited by Aquinas, treats of domestic rule—in St. Thomas' words, of economic subjection. In the 16th chapter St. Augustine regards the family as an important unit in the wider rule of the city. This passage,

---

[42]*S.T.*, Ia, q. 96, art. 4, c: Si unus homo habuisset super alios supereminentiam scientiae et justitiae, inconveniens fuisset, nisi hoc exequeretur in utilitatem aliorum.

[43]Cf. *S.T.*, Ia-IIae, q. 72, art. 4, c: Triplex autem ordo in homine debet esse: unus quidem secundum comparationem ad regulam rationis. . .alius autem ordo est per comparationem ad regulam divinae legis. . .Tertius ordo, quo homo ordinetur hic ad alios homines, quibus convivere debet.

[44]*S.T.*, Ia, q. 96, art. 4, c: Si unus homo habuisset super alios supereminentiam scientiae. . .Unde Augustinus dicit *(De Civ. Dei*, lib. XIX, cap. 14, in fin.), quod 'justi non dominandi cupiditate imperant, sed officio consulendi;' et cap: 15: 'Hoc naturalis ordo praescribit; ita Deus hominem condidit.'

because of its probable influence upon Aquinas, may well
be quoted:

> Every family then being part of the city,
> every beginning having relation unto some end,
> and every part tending to the integrity of the
> whole, it follows apparently, that the family's
> peace adheres unto the city's, that is, the orderly
> command, and obedience in the family, has real
> reference to the orderly rule and subjection in the
> city. So that the 'father of the family' may fetch
> his instructions from the city's government,
> whereby he may proportionate the peace of his
> private estate, by that of the common.[45]

Such a conception of the family was close to that held by
Aquinas; and such a conception of the family was embodied in the thirteenth-century seigniory. The thirteenth-
century rural family with its wide range of relations and
cooperation existing among its members was a strongly
ordered group and a true cell of society.

b) The Science of Household Management and the Art
of Natural Wealth-Getting

St. Thomas' economics, unlike much of our contemporary economic thought that has divorced itself from
Scholasticism, is based upon teleological considerations.[46]
Economic functions were evaluated in terms of the ends or
purposes they served. These functions originally were so
bound up with the needs of a particular group—the domestic group—that they were denominated according to the
end they served, namely, the good life of the household

---

[45]*City of God*, Bk. XIX, chap. 16, unabridged ed; or Bk. XV,
chap. 16, Dent abridged ed.

[46]Cf. Tawney, R. H., *Religion and the Rise of Capitalism*, New
York: Harcourt Brace, 1926, p. 191.

group.[47] *Oeconomica,* was the science of household management.[48] The function of wealth-getting, in its natural form, is closely associated with this science.[49]

St. Thomas' notions of household management show a marked influence of Aristotle, whose teaching on this subject St. Thomas accepted, enlarged upon, and clarified in his commentaries on the *Politics,* the *Ethics,* as also in his *Summa Theologica. Oeconomica* is a virtue, a species of prudence. It stands between political prudence and individual prudence just as the household stands midway between the state and the person.[50] Prudence, absolutely speaking, is ordained to one's own good: household management is ordained to the common good of the household or the family: political prudence is ordained to the common good of the state.[51] The end of *oeconomica* is to live well, according to domestic relationship. Riches are but the instruments to achieve this higher good.[52]

It needs hardly to be pointed out that *oeconomica* is not peculiar to the rural domestic group. Since it is the proper activity of this virtue prudently to dispense natural riches in the household, rather than to acquire them, it is

---

[47]Cf. *S.T.,* IIa-IIae, q. 50, art. 3, ad 1: Finis autem ultimus oeconomicae est totum bene vivere, secundum domesticam conversationem.

[48]Cf. *Politics,* Bk. I, chap. 3; *In Polit.,* Bk. I, lect. 8; *S.T.,* IIa-IIae, q. 47, art. 11; q. 50, art. 3.

[49]Cf. *In Polit.,* Bk. I, lect. 8.

[50]Cf. *S.T.,* IIa-IIae, q. 50, art. 3: Oeconomica est species prudentiae, media inter politicam et prudentiam quae ad unius regimen est ordinata.

[51]*S.T.,* IIa-IIae, q. 47, art. 11: Una sit prudentia simpliciter dicta, quae ordinatur ad bonum proprium; alia autem oeconomica quae ordinatur ad bonum commune domus, vel familiae; et tertia politica, quae ordinatur ad bonum commune civitatis, vel regni. Cf. also *In Ethic.,* I, 1, for threefold division of moral philosophy into *monastica, oeconomica,* and *politica.*

[52]Cf. *S.T.,* IIa-IIae, q. 50, art. 3, ad 1: Divitiae comparantur ad oeconomicam, non sicut finis ultimus, sed sicut instrumenta quaedam, ut dicitur (*Polit.* lib. 1, cap. 5 et 7).

evident that it may be practiced in the urban household even though the practice of agriculture be no part of its activity. Yet, a further study of Thomistic texts on this point will reveal a very close connection between this science and the art of wealth-getting from the bounties of nature. In practice this close connection is realized only in the rural household, and in the urban household that carries on a part-time agriculture. That such was the thought of St. Thomas on this question becomes more evident when the historical background is taken into account. Actually most households were on the land, and many even of those that were not on the land practiced a part-time agriculture, as was the case in thirteenth-century Italy.[53]

1) Relation of Natural Wealth-Getting to *Oeconomica*

The proper object of *oeconomica*, as also of *politica*, is not to acquire food, but to dispense it either in the household or in the state.[54] The productivity of nature, which effects the generation of men and of articles of food, and the art of wealth-getting, which husbands these fruits of nature, are directed to the needs of those who manage the household. In the words of Aquinas, these "zealously serve" *oeconomica*.[55]

The statements of St. Thomas on the art of wealth-getting, like his statements on *oeconomica*, also point to the close, though subservient, relationship between this art and the science of *oeconomica*. Aristotle had said that natural riches and the natural art of wealth-getting are part of the

---

[53]Cf. *above*, chap. II, 3, a.

[54]*In Polit.*, I, 8: Acquirere...cibum non est proprium opus et immediatum politicae vel oeconomicae: sed proprium opus eius est dispensare ista in domo, sicut oportet.

[55]*Ibid.*: Sic igitur oeconomicae deservit et natura, quae generat homines et cibus, iterum pecuniativa, quae acquirit.

management of a household; but he placed a distinction upon this statement, adding: "in their true form they are part of the management of a household."[56]   These are thus distinguished from retail trade which is "the art of producing wealth, not in every way, but by exchange."[57]   This form of the art of wealth-getting seeks riches to which there are no limits: "and there is no bound to the riches which spring from this art of wealth-getting."[58]   For like any art it tends to accomplish its end to the utmost.   In this it stands in contrast to necessary wealth-getting: "but the art of wealth-getting which consists in household management, on the other hand, has a limit; the unlimited acquisition of wealth is not its business."[59]   About these two forms of wealth-getting Aristotle reaches the following conclusions:

> Thus, then, we have considered the art of wealth-getting which is unnecessary, and why men want it; and also the necessary art of wealth-getting, which we have seen to be different from the other, and to be a natural part of the art of managing a household, concerned with the provision of

---

[56]*Polit.*, Bk. I, chap. 9, 1257b, 20. By the true form of natural riches and wealth-getting Aristotle understands first, the acquisition of that property given by nature itself to all, for a bare livelihood, *Polit.*, Bk. I, chap. 8, 1256b, 7ff., for food, for clothing, and for various instruments, *Polit.*, Bk. I, chap. 8, 1256b, 15; and secondly, simple barter, *Polit.*, Bk. I, chap. 9, 1257a, 40 ff, which is needed for the satisfaction of man's natural wants, *Polit.*, Bk. I, chap. 9, 1257a, 28.

[57]*Polit.*, Bk. I, chap. 9, 1257b, 21-2.

[58]*Polit.*, Bk. I, chap. 9, 1257b, 23-30. In, *Polit.*, Bk. I, chap. 9, 1258a, 5, Aristotle, with accurate insight into the human heart, explains why men seek riches without limit. Not knowing how to live well, some think that enjoyments must be had in excess. For this they need an excess of wealth of the spurious kind, and use every means to obtain wealth, and turn every personal quality, or art, into getting wealth.

[59]*Polit.*, Bk. I, chap. 9, 1257b, 30-33.

food, not, however, like the former kind, unlimited, but having a limit.[60]

St. Thomas develops Aristotle's basic notions of the art of wealth-getting, both in itself and in its relation to the science of household management. The art of wealth-getting, as it is practiced by those who husband the fruits of nature that the latter may sustain the life of man, is natural. Husbandmen are carrying out the order of nature:

> Nature neither leaves anything imperfect, nor does anything in vain; therefore it is manifest that nature makes animals and plants that these may sustain the life of men. And when anyone acquires that which nature has made for him, this is a natural acquisition.[61]

2) Unnatural Wealth-Getting

To understand St. Thomas' emphasis upon this natural form of wealth-getting in its relation to the household, it will be necessary to explain briefly the other form of wealth-getting of which he speaks, namely, exchange for gain *(lucrum)*. Commenting on the *Politics*, he distinguishes two forms of wealth-getting:[62] one of which is called *campsoria,* which acquires wealth from wealth and on account of wealth itself; the other form is that which acquires riches from natural things, from fruits and ani-

---

[60]*Polit.*, Bk. I, chap. 9, 1258a, 14-19.

[61]*In Polit.*, I, 6: Sed natura, neque dimittit aliquid imperfectum, neque facit aliquid frustra; ergo manifestum est quod natura fecit animalia et plantas ad sustentationem hominum. Sed quando aliquis acquirit id quod natura propter ipsum fecit, est naturalis acquisitio. (The English translations of all passages from the *Commentary on the Politics* are by the writer.)

[62]St. Thomas' treatment of this point is far clearer than that of Aristotle, since the latter does not distinguish as carefully between the forms of wealth-getting and the forms of trading as does St. Thomas.

mals.[63] This latter form, according to St. Thomas, "pertains to household management... is necessary for the life of man ... is praiseworthy."[64]   The first form, namely *nummularia* (or *campsoria)*

> is an outgrowth of that which is a necessity of nature, and has now developed into that which concupiscence requires, as was said above, and therefore is justly condemned. This form of wealth-getting is not according to nature, because is does not come from natural things, nor is it directed to supplying the necessities of nature.[65]

When wealth-getting is directed to the needs of the household—a condition which was realized in the 13th-century husbandman's wealth-getting activities—it has, in these needs, a natural principle of limitation and control. When, on the contrary, it is directed to no end outside itself, as happens with *campsoria*, then the acquisition will go on indefinitely toward an ever receding end.   St. Thomas presents this argument in strict form, thus:

> The pursuing of an end in any art is without limit: the pursuing of that, however, which has a relation to some end, is not without limit, but has a limit set by the rule and measure of that end; as the art of medicine aims at healing without limit, since it induces healing wheresoever it can.
> But wealth is related to *pecuniativam campsoriam*, as an end: for this form seeks to acquire

---

[63]Cf. *In Polit.*, I, 8.

[64]*In Polit.*, I, 8: Alia autem pecuniativa est oeconomica, quae scilicet acquirit pecunias ex rebus naturalibus...ista...est necessaria ad vitam hominum, unde et laudatum.

[65]*Ibid.*: Alia vero, scilicet nummularia, transfertur ad eo quod est necessarium naturae ad id quod requirit concupiscentia, ut supra dictum est, et ideo juste vituperatur; non enim illa pecuniativa est secundum naturam, quia neque ex rebus naturalibus est, neque ad supplendam necessitatem naturae ordinatur.

wealth. On the other hand, wealth is related to household management, not as an end, but as something ordered to an end, which is the management of the home.

Therefore, wealth-getting seeks wealth without limit, whereas, household management seeks it in a limited degree.[66]

The inordinate pursuing of wealth is to be attributed, as was noted above, to man's concupiscence. St. Thomas distinguishes two kinds of concupiscence; the one limited, the other without limit. It is the second kind that gives rise to inordinate wealth-getting. He finds occasion, while explaining these two kinds of concupiscence, to repeat and enlarge upon the argument in the *Politics* that wealth-getting divorced from the legitimate needs of the household will go on without limit.

Another reason may be assigned, according to the Philosopher *(Polit.* 1, 3), why a certain concupiscence is finite, and another infinite. Because concupiscence of the end is always infinite: since the end is desired for its own sake, e.g., health: and thus greater health is more desired, and so on to infinity. . . On the other hand, concupiscence of the means is not infinite, because the concupiscence of the means is in suitable proportion to the end. Consequently, those who place their end in riches have an infinite concupiscence of riches; whereas those who desire riches, on account of the necessities of life, desire a finite measure of riches,

---

[66]*In Polit.*, Bk. I, lect. 8: Desiderium finis in unaquaque arte est in infinitum: desiderium autem ejus, quod est ad finem, non est in infinitum, sed habet terminum secundum regulam et mensuram finis; sicut ars medicinalis intendit ad sanandum in infinitum, cum inducit sanitatem quamcumque potest; sed pecuniae se habent ad pecuniativam campsoriam, sicut finis, haec enim intendit acquirere pecunias. Ad oeconomicam autem non se habent sicut finis, sed sicut ordinatum ad finem qui est gubernatio domus; ergo pecuniativa quaerit pecunias absque termino, oeconomica autem cum aliquo termino.

sufficient for the necessities of life, as the Philosopher says *(ibid.)*.[67]

It is therefore a cardinal principle in St. Thomas' philosophy that wealth-getting activities must take their ordering from ends that are outside and above them. His approach is teleological throughout. He looked upon the natural and limited needs of the household for bodily goods as a very important control over wealth-getting activities. Consequently, it may be said that those households, such as the rural domestic group, and the urban domestic group which carried on part-time husbandry, where in both instances the wealth-getting activity was directed to the immediate needs of the various particular households, were for this reason very important groups from an economic viewpoint. Only in the case of the domestic group on the land does there exist that immediate relation between production and consumption which makes need the measure of production. These rural groups provided in good measure that control over wealth-producing activities demanded by the Thomistic synthesis. And this is true not only for the household of the lord of the 13th-century seigniory, but it was also realized in the households of the dependent cultivators. These latter, because they possessed a sizeable plot of land which they cultivated independently for themselves, were also ordered in their wealth-getting activity. Many advan-

---

[67]*S.T.*, Ia-IIae, q. 20, art. 4, c: Potest et alia ratio assignari secundum Philosophum (*Politic.* lib. 1, cap. 6, post med.), quare quaedam concupiscentia sit finita et quaedam infinita. Semper enim concupiscentia finis est infinita; finis enim per se concupiscitur, ut sanitas; unde major sanitas magis concupiscitur, et sic in infinitum...Concupiscentia vero ejus quod est ad finem, non est infinita, si secundum illam mensuram appetitur, quae convenit fini. Unde qui finem ponunt in divitiis, habent concupiscentiam divitiarum in infinitum; qui autem divitias appetunt propter necessitatem vitae, concupiscunt divitias finitas sufficientes ad necessitatem vitae, ut Philosophus dicit (*ibid.*).

tages flowed from this sound socio-economic ordering: families enjoyed security in the obtaining of the necessities of life; traffic in foodstuffs was kept at a minimum; and society was spared the obligation of meeting the costs of numerous middle men and of excessive transportation handling and storage charges.

3. THE RURAL OCCUPATIONAL GROUP

As man's social nature gives rise to the domestic group, so also it demands the political group. These two groups are fundamental, and are frequently given joint mention by St. Thomas.[68] The occupational group falls within the latter of these two. It has been shown that the 13th-century rural domestic group possessed the constituents of true order and contributed much to the social and economic ordering of man. This cell of society gave strength to the state or principality. Aquinas recognized the necessity of other groups within the principality arising from a "diversity of offices and actions." The question therefore arises whether the rural life of his day, which was conducive to domestic grouping, also lent itself to this occupational grouping that he required for a sound state or principality.

St. Thomas defines the principality as "one multitude ordered in one way under the rule of a prince."[69] A multitude is said to be "ordered in one way," when it can be governed by the same set of laws and is under one administration. This condition is realized in one city:

---

[68]Cf. *S.T.*, Ia, q. 92, art. 1, ad 2; *S.T.*, Ia-IIae, q. 87, art. 1, c; *S.T.*, Ia-IIae, q. 104, art. 4, c.

[69]*S.T.*, Ia, q. 108, art. 2, c: Una hierarchia est unus principatus, id est, una multitudo ordinata uno modo sub principis gubernatione. In the usage of St. Thomas, hierarchy means a sacred principality. *S.T.*, Ia, q. 108, art. 1, c: Hierarchia est sacer principatus...In nomine autem principatus duo intelliguntur, scilicet ipse princeps, et multitudo ordinata sub principe.

But if we consider the principality on the part of the multitude ordered under the prince, then principality is said to be one according as the multitude can be subject in one way to the government of the prince. And those that cannot be governed in the same way by a prince belong to different principalities; thus, under one king there are different cities, which are governed by different laws and administrators.[70]

a) Orders within the Principality

If confusion is to be avoided within any principality, St. Thomas continues, then it is necessary that its members be divided into different orders, according to a diversity of offices and actions:

Now such a multitude (principality) would not be ordered, but confused, if there were not in it different orders. So the nature of a hierarchy requires diversity of orders. This diversity of orders arises from the diversity of offices and actions, as appears in one city where there are different orders according to the different actions.[71]

---

[70]*S.T.*, Ia, q. 108, art. 1, c: Sed si consideretur principatus ex parte multitudinis ordinatae sub principe, sic unus principatus dicitur secundum quod multitudo uno et eodem modo potest gubernationem principis recipere. Quae vero non possunt secundum eumdem modum gubernari a principe, ad diversos principatus pertinent; sicut sub uno rege sunt diversae civitates, quae diversis reguntur legibus et ministris.

[71]*S.T.*, Ia, q. 108, art. 2, c: Non autem esset multitudo ordinata, sed confusa, si in multitudine diversi ordines non essent. Ipsa ergo ratio hierarchiae requirit ordinum diversitatem. Quae quidem diversitas ordinum secundum diversa officia et actus consideratur, sicut patet quod in una civitate sunt diversi ordines secundum diversos actus.

Also *In Sent.* II, d. 9, art. 3, c: Diversitas vero ordinum est secundum diversos actus.

"Civitas" refers to the city-state. In the previous articles it signified one multitude under one set of laws and one administrator.

He enumerates certain of these orders[72] that may be found in the city comprising one rule: "For there is one order of those who judge, and another of those who fight, and another of those who labor in the fields, and so forth."[73] This list of orders is clearly not exhaustive, as the text itself indicates. Further light is thrown on the meaning of the word "order," as used here, St. Thomas' use of this word in his discussion on the functional relations existing among the angels. And inasmuch as he uses a common terminology when writing of orders, whether these be among men or angels, his use of the word "order" in the context of angelology will be pertinent to the present discussion. In one passage he compares the functions of the angelic orders with the functions of the parallel orders in the human hierarchy. In this passage he refers to the order among men that attends to the execution of a law;[74] and to the order of the master-builder who directs skilled workers.[75] Here St. Thomas also states that in any one order there is a diversity of persons according to their differing strength in the execution of an act more or less efficacious.[76] The immediate application of this statement is to an angelic order but, since St. Thomas is here comparing an angelic

---

[72]Here "order" is to be taken in its concrete sense, as signifying a group of those who are of one rank. St. Thomas distinguishes this use of the word from its abstract use as signifying an ordination between different ranks: *In Sent.* II, d. 9, q. 1, ad 2: Ordo potest sumi dupliciter: vel secundum quod nominat unum gradum tantum, sicut qui sunt unius gradus, dicuntur unius ordinis; et sic ordo est pars hierarchiae: vel secundum quod nominat relationem quae est inter diversos gradus, ut ordo dicatur ipsa ordinatio; et sic sumitur quasi abstracte. Cf. also *S.T.*, Ia, q. 108, art. 2, ad 1.

[73]*S.T.*, Ia, q. 108, art. 2, c: Nam alius est ordo judicantium, et alius pugnantium, et alius laborantium in agris, et sic de aliis.

[74]Cf. *In Sent.* II, d. 9, 3, c: ...Sicut et leges saeculares oportet esse armatos, ut habeant vim coactivam.

[75]Cf. *Ibid.*: sicut architector in mechanicis qui...est praeceptivus.

[76]Cf. *Ibid.*: ...secundum diversam virtutem in executione actus minus vel magis efficaci.

order to an order of men, it is probable that it may also be applied to any order among men. Thus even among the master-builders who form one order there would be differences because of their differing abilities.

b) The Agrarian Occupational Order

The orders, arising from a "diversity of offices and actions" are clearly occupational groups. The relation obtaining among the members is based upon their common occupation, whether this be judging, or directing craftsmen, or laboring in the fields. However, to identify these occupational groups, with the "vocational groups" of the social encyclical does not seem to be justified on the basis of the texts considered above. These latter represent groups formed by a vertical division of society according to a common occupation, e.g., the building trade including architects and skilled workers.[77] Taken literally, the order "of those who labor in the fields," would signify only the laborers within the agricultural vocational group, and exclude the overseers and the rural lords. In like manner the order "of those who fight" might be taken to refer to those who fight under the order of a lord of prince. Again, the master-craftsman would seem to be in a different order than the skilled laborer in that same craft. Thus "order" in the present context is best taken to signify that group, of one

---

[77]This is the "vocational group" of Pius XI's, *Quadragesimo Anno*, where it is written that "the aim of social legislation must therefore be the re-establishment of vocational groups." par. 82, Nell-Breuning-Dempsey text, in, *Reorganization of Social Economy*, Milwaukee: Bruce, 1936-7, p. 423. Of these groups Nell-Breuning writes: "Let us, again, start with the order in one vocational group. There is no lack of multiplicity! The members of the guild add their share of professional activity, as a contribution to the welfare of the whole, in most varied manner. Every profession requires directive and executive activity, planning and thinking as well as doing." pp. 226-7.

rank, which is engaged in the same occupation. The order "of those who labor in the fields" comprises those of one rank who are engaged in agriculture.

The difficulty is mainly one of terminology. According to St. Thomas, it is part of the beauty of order that there should be a natural inequality among men.[78] Elsewhere, speaking of the beauty of order within the Church he writes that this is obtained because men take their places in different ranks or grades within the exercise of the same office.[79] It is entirely in keeping with the thought of St. Thomas—indeed it seems to be demanded by it—that the various orders, signifying groups of those who are of one rank or grade, should cooperate on different levels of function in those things belonging to their common occupation, with a view toward the attainment of a common end.[80] This would be the "vocational group" of the encyclical *Quadragesimo Anno*. Following this interpretation, the order "of those who labor in the fields" is a part of the agricultural "vocational group", as conceived by the encyclical.

A study of the historical background of Aquinas' time throws some light on this obscure and isolated reference to the order "of those who labor in the fields". It is a matter of fact that the peasants of St. Thomas' time did form a

---

[78]Cf. *S.T.*, Ia, q .96, art. 3, ad 3: Causa disparitatis poterat esse ex parte Dei...ut pulchritudo ordinis magis in hominibus reluceret. Cf. also, *above*, Chap. IV, sect. 1, p. 78, on the element of *distinctio* in order.

[79]Cf. *S.T.*, IIa-IIae, q. 183, art. 3, c: Alia autem (distinctio diversitatis fidelium) per respectum ad ordinem pulchritudinis ecclesiasticae: et secundum hoc accipitur differentia graduum, prout scilicet etiam in eodem...officio unus est alio superior.

[80]Cf. *In Div. Nom.*, IV, 1, on distinction as a condition of order; *S.T.*, Ia, q. 96, art. 4, on the fittingness that some should direct; Ostheimer, A. L., *The Family*, Washington: Catholic University of America Press, 1939, pp. 173-6, on "Vocational Groups in Thomistic Social Organization"; Cox, J. F., *op. cit.*, pp. 73ff., "The Vocational Group".

group that was organized on the basis of common occupation, and one that possessed those constituents of true social order demanded by him. Whether the peasants were organized on the basis of the seigniory, or, where the village was not part of a seigniory, on the basis of one village, in both cases they had a common end, and cooperated according to their different offices in attaining that end.

The historical facts of this agrarian cooperation having been presented in a preceding chapter,[81] need only be touched upon here. The peasants cooperated through a common use of waste land, forest land, and natural resources. The three-course open-field system required intricate planning and cooperation in the matter of crop rotation, of fallowing, of the use of those fields for grazing where the season's crops had been removed. The prohibition of private hedges illustrates this type of cooperation. The planning required for this cooperative husbandry was done through the village meeting. Again, use of the lord's equipment and machinery, or the use of machinery owned in common by the peasants, helped to solve the problem of limited capital. Where the peasants were part of a seigniory, they were able to benefit by the lord's greater prestige, technical knowledge, and ability to organize husbandry, and by his authority to keep order.

c) The Recognition of Custom in Rural Cooperation

The orderly and equitable cooperation of the peasants was insured through local customs that had the force of law. Such were the customs stabilizing the days of labor, and the amount of produce or money due to the lord; and such was the *lex et consuetudo marisci* that protected individual rights on the commons. It is clear that these local customs would not have arisen, nor would they have been

---

[81] Cf. *above*, Chap. II, sect. 2.

able to impose obligations, unless the peasants had become
accustomed to cooperate in their husbandry for a common
good.

That custom should have the force of a law is clearly in
accord with the teaching of St. Thomas: "custom has the
force of a law, abolishes law, and is the interpreter of law."[82]
His argument, in general, is that a law derives from the
reason and will of the legislator, which can be manifested
as well by act as by word.   Now, since the word of man, in
so far as it is an expression of man's reason, can change a
law, in like manner it can be changed by customary acts.

> Wherefore by actions also, especially if they
> be repeated, so as to make a custom, law can be
> changed and expounded; and also something can
> be established which obtains force of law, in so far
> as by repeated external actions, the inward move-
> ment of the will, and concepts of reason are most
> effectually declared.[83]

St. Thomas anticipates an objection in regard to his teaching on the force of custom, namely, that it belongs to those
who rule the community to create laws.   In answer St.
Thomas states that the community does not surrender its
rights to the ruler unconditionally.   The latter has the
right to legislate only in so far as he stands for the
community.

> For if they are free, and able to make their
> own laws, the consent of the whole people ex-
> pressed by a custom counts far more in favour

---

[82]*S.T.*, Ia-IIae, q. 97, art. 3, c: Consuetudo et habet vim legis, et
legem abolet, et est legum interpretatrix.

[83]*S.T.*, Ia-IIae, q. 97, art. 3, c: Unde etiam et per actus maxime
multiplicatos, qui consuetudinem efficiunt, mutari potest lex, et ex-
poni, et etiam aliquid causari quod legis virtutem obtineat; inquantum scilicet per exteriores actus multiplicatos interior voluntatis motus, et rationis conceptus efficacissime declaratur.

of a particular observance, than does the authority
of the sovereign, who has not the power to frame
laws, except as representing the people.[84]

Accordingly, custom protected the rights of the individual
peasants, both when they cooperated among themselves,
and also when they cultivated dependently upon the lord.

It is to be noted that the agrarian occupational group
of the 13th century possessed an ordering that went beyond
that due to their common occupation. By reason of the
seigniorial organization the peasants partook also of the
lord's domestic order. Thus the peasants in their relation
to the lord came, in varying degrees, under his domestic
authority; and also in relation to the lord they had a part
in the common agricultural enterprise of the seigniory.
And over and above this, in their village life, they cooperated in agriculture and its associated crafts. Whatever may
be said of the evils of 13th-century agrarian life, it cannot
be denied that this life was organized on the natural bases
of family and occupation. For this reason, it contributed
much to the order of the principality.

4. SELF-SUFFICIENCY IN THE VARIOUS SOCIAL GROUPS

It is part of man's social nature that he should live in
groups, and through group activities to compensate for his

---

[84]*S.T.*, Ia-IIae, q. 97, art. 3, ad 3: Plus est consensus totius multitudinis ad aliquid observandum, quod consuetudo manifestat, quam
auctoritas Principis, qui non habet potestatem condendi legum, nisi
inquantum gerit personam multitudinis. Moreover, custom can also
obtain the force of law even though "the people have not the free
power to make their own laws, or to abolish a law made by a higher
authority." *Ibid.*: Si vero multitudo non habeat liberam potestatem
condendi sibi legem vel legem a superiori potestate positam removen-
di, tamen ipsa consuetudo in tali multitudine praevalens obtinet vim
legis, inquantum per eos toleratur ad quos pertinet multitudini legem
imponere; ex hoc enim ipso videntur approbare quod consuetudo in-
troduxit.

deficiencies as an individual. To each of these groups in which man has a natural membership there belongs a certain sufficiency in the procurement of the necessities of life:

> There is, indeed, to some extent sufficiency for life in one family of one household, namely in so far as pertains to the natural acts of nourishment and the begetting of offspring and other things of this kind; it exists, furthermore, in one village with regard to those things which belong to one trade; but it exists in a city, which is a perfect community, with regard to all the necessities of life; but still more in a province because of the need of fighting together and of mutual help against enemies.[85]

Within certain general limits, the ends of these natural socio-economic groups must be respected. The end that is proper to the family, for example, should be left for it to attain. This end should not be taken over by the state and made one of its functions. In like manner with the village in reference to the city; and the city in reference to the province. Should it come about, that the purpose served by any smaller group were to be taken over by a larger one, then the group itself would cease to exist, inasmuch as the end is the ultimate determinant of the unity and being of any group. But what precisely Aquinas considers to be the limits of self-sufficiency attainable by these several groups cannot be determined from this text alone. In fact, such limits would vary from century to century with changes in the technique of production and transportation. Limits

---

[85]*The Governance of Rulers*, Phelan trans. of the *De Reg. Princ*, pp. 38-9; *De Reg. Princ.*, I, I: Habetur siquidem aliqua vitae sufficientia, in una familia domus unius, quantum scilicet ad naturales actus nutritionis, et prolis generandae, et aliorum hujusmodi; in uno autem vico, quantum ad ea quae ad unum artificium pertinent; in civitate vero, quae est perfecta communitas, quantum ad omnia necessaria vitae; sed adhuc magis in provincia una propter necessitatem compugnationis et mutui auxilii contra hostes.

valid in the 13th century would have little meaning in a later century. Of more importance than any such detailed enumerations of the functions proper to each of these groups are the general principles by which Aquinas gauges the ends proper to them. These are valid for any age.

a) Self-sufficiency for the City-Country Unit

One of these is the principle that may well be called the principle of self-sufficiency, namely, that self-sufficiency is a mark of perfection: "the higher a thing is the more self-suffcient it is; since whatever needs another's help is by that fact proven inferior."[86] St. Thomas had used this principle in support of his suggestion to King Hugh of Cyprus, to whom he addresses the *De Regimine Principum*, that he should aim to make his city self-sufficient in the matter of food, through the produce obtainable from the surrounding fields. It is better, writes Aquinas, to have the city supplied in this manner, rather than through trade:

> Now there are two ways in which an abundance of food-stuffs can be supplied to a city. The first we have already mentioned, where the soil is so fertile that it richly provides for all the necessities of human life. The second is by trade, through which the necessaries of life are brought to the town from different places. But it is quite clear that the first means is better. For the higher a thing is the more self-sufficient it is; since whatever needs another's help is by that fact proven inferior. But that city is more self-sufficient which the surrounding country supplies with all its vital needs, than is another which must obtain these supplies by trade.[87]

[86]*The Governance of Rulers*, pp. 116-7; *De Reg. Princ.*, II, 3: Tanto enim aliquid dignius est, quanto per se sufficientius invenitur, quia quod alio indiget, deficiens esse monstratur.

[87]*The Governance of Rulers*, pp. 116-7; *De Reg. Princ.*, II, 3: Duo autem sunt modi, quibus alicui civitati potest affluentia rerum

Moreover, the self-sufficient city is more dignified; and in
time of war it is safer:

> A city which has an abundance of food from
> its own territory is more dignified than one which
> is provisioned by merchants. It is safer, too, it
> seems. For, the importing of supplies can easily
> be prevented, whether owing to the uncertain out-
> come of wars or to the many dangers of the roads,
> and thus the city may be overcome through lack
> of food.[88]

suppetere. Unus qui dictus est propter regionis fertilitatem abunde
omnia producentis quae humanae vitae requirit necessitas. Alius
autem per mercationis usum, ex quo ibidem necessaria vitae ex diversis partibus adducantur. Primus autem motus convenientior esse
manifeste convincitur. Tanto enim aliquid dignius est, quanto per
se sufficientius invenitur, quia quod alio indiget, deficiens esse monstratur. Sufficientiam autem plenius possidet civitas, cui circumjacens regio sufficiens est ad necessaria vitae, quam illa quae indiget
ab aliis per mercationem accipere.

[88]*Ibid.:* Dignior enim est civitas si abundantiam rerum habeat ex
territorio proprio, quam si per mercatores abundet. Cum hoc etiam
videtur esse securius, quia propter bellorum eventus et diversa viarum
discrimina, de facili potest impedire victualium deportatio, et sic
civitas per defectum victualium opprimetur. *In Polit.*, VII, 4, a portion of the commentary now generally regarded as spurious, self-
sufficiency in foodstuffs is urged for the city. It is stated that the
territory surrounding the city will merit praise if it is sufficient to
provide all those things that are needed for the good life—"quae sunt
necessaria ad bene vivere." By its fertility the surrounding land
should provide the requisite food and drink. Again with a view to
self-sufficiency, the region surrounding the city should be examined
for its arable and grazing land. This condition of self-sufficiency is
desirable that men may live "according to virtue." The interesting
observation is also made that foodstuffs should be at hand that man
may use them temperately in satisfaction of his own needs, and liberally in regard to the needs of others. St. Thomas points out elsewhere—*S.T.*, IIa-IIae, q. 141, art. 6, ad 3—that "temperance regards
need according to the requirements of life, and this depends not only
on the requirements of the body, but also on the requirements of external things, such as riches and station, and more still on the requirements of good conduct."

b) Traders in the City

St. Thomas, while clearly favoring the self-sufficient city, does not entirely rule out the work of the trader. The significance of his social philosophy is in the balance that it strikes between the ideal of self-sufficiency, on the one hand, and the exigencies of the city for some trade, on the other. The well-ordered city or state will depend upon merchants in a moderate degree:

> Traders must not be entirely kept out of a city, since one cannot easily find any place so overflowing with all the necessaries of life as not to need some commodities from other lands. In the same way, if there is an over-abundance of some commodities in that place, this would cause loss to many if the surplus could not be carried to other lands by professional traders. Consequently, the perfect city will make a moderate use of merchants.[89]

This rule is such as to allow, on the one hand for a good standard of living through the influx of outside goods into the city; and to prevent, on the other, those social and economic evils arising when too many traders dwell there.

The presence of many traders has a corrupting influence upon civic life; and this is particularly true if the traders are foreigners. For, as Aquinas points out, "intercourse with foreigners, according to Aristotle's *Politics*, is particularly harmful to civic customs."[90] But it is also true when the traders are citizens:

---

[89]*The Governance of Rulers*, pp. 118-9; *De Reg. Princ.*, II, 3: Nec tamen negotiatores omnino a civitate oportet excludi, quia non de facili potest inveniri locus qui sic omnibus vitae necessariis abundet, quod non indigeat aliquibus aliunde allatis, eorumque quae in eodem loco superabundant, eodem modo reddetur multis damnosa copia, si per mercatorum officium ad alia loca transferri non possent. Unde oportet quod perfecta civitas moderate mercatoribus utatur.

[90]*The Governance of Rulers*, p. 117; *De Reg. Princ.*, II, 3: Extraneorum autem conversatio corrumpit plurimum civium mores, secundum Aristotelis doctrinam in sua *Politica*.

Again, if the citizens themselves devote their lives to matters of trade, the way will be opened to many vices. For, since the object of tradesmen leads especially to making money, greed is awakened in the hearts of the citizens through the pursuit of trade. The result is that everything in the city will be offered for sale: confidence will be destroyed and the way opened to all kinds of trickery: each one will work only for his own profit, despising the public good; the cultivation of virtue will fail, since honour, virtue's reward, will be bestowed upon anybody. Thus, in such a city civic life will necessarily be corrupted.[91]

Where there are many traders, wealth-getting activity of a spurious kind—the end of which is mere gain—will prevail. "Everything in the city will be offered for sale." The emphasis will be on exchange-value rather than on use-value. Men will be more concerned with profit than with the fulfillment of the natural needs of the public.

Such being the evils attendant upon excessive trade, the wise ruler will follow a policy whereby the city will be provisioned from its neighboring fields, a policy "more conducive to civic life."[92] This appears to have been the policy of the 13th-century Italian town of Viterbo, which encouraged a direct exchange of foodstuffs and of other goods or money between the town and its immediate countryside;[93] and the policy of 13th-century Padua and

---

[91]*The Governance of Rulers*, pp. 117-8; *De Reg. Princ.*, II, 3: Rursus, si cives ipsi mercationibus fuerint dediti, pandetur pluribus vitiis aditus. Nam cum negotiatorum studium maxime ad lucrum tendat per negotiationis usum, cupiditas in cordibus civium traducitur, ex quo convenit ut in civitate omnia fiant venalia, et fide substracta, locus fraudibus aperitur, publicoque bono contempto, proprio commodo quisque deserviet, deficietque virtutis studium, dum honor virtutis praemium omnibus deferetur: unde necesse erit in tali civitate civilem conversationem corrumpi.

[92]*The Governance of Rulers*, p. 117; *De Reg. Princ.*, II, 3: Est etiam hoc utilius ad conservationem civilem.

[93]Cf. *above*, chap. II, sect. 3.

Sambuca, which insisted upon a certain amount of intense cultivation of land in the suburban district.[94] The part-time farming of the inhabitants of Chieri achieved the same results.[95]

Just as Aquinas distinguishes the wealth-getting of the husbandman that is natural, from that unnatural form of wealth-getting which seeks to make money from money, so he also distinguishes two forms of trading, having first defined the tradesman as one whose business consists in the exchange of things. One form of trading, whereby one commodity is exchanged for another, or money taken in exchange for a commodity, in order to satisfy the needs of life, is natural, as it were, and necessary. This form, properly speaking, does not belong to tradesmen, but rather to those who have care of the home, or to civil servants, who have to provide, respectively, the household or the state with the necessaries of life. The other kind of exchange is either that of money for money, or of any commodity for money, not on account of the necessities of life, but for profit, and this kind of exchange, properly speaking, pertains to tradesmen. The former kind of exchange is regarded by St. Thomas as commendable because it supplies a natural need: but the latter is justly deserving of blame, because, considered in itself, it satisfied the greed for gain, which knows no limit and tends to infinity. Hence trading, considered in itself has a certain debasement attaching thereto, in so far as by its very nature it does not imply a virtuous or necessary end.[96]

---

[94]Cf. *above*, chap. II, sect. 3.

[95]Cf. *Ibid.*

[96]Cf. *S.T.*, IIa-IIae, q. 77, art. 4, c: Ad negotiatores pertinet commutationibus rerum insistere. Ut autem Philosophus dicit (*Polit.* lib. 1, cap. 5 et 6), duplex est rerum commutatio: una quidem quasi naturalis et necessaria; per quam scilicet fit commutatio rei ad rem, vel rerum et denariorum propter necessitatem vitae, et talis commutatio non proprie pertinet ad negotiatores, sed magis ad oeconomicos, vel politicos, qui habent providere vel domui vel civitati de rebus ne-

Obviously, the trading described as that which pertains to the one who has care of the home is closely related to *oeconomica,* just as is the acquisition of natural wealth. It is directed "to satisfy the needs of life." For this reason it is natural and limited by a fixed end. Such was the trading in the thirteenth-century Italian town markets, carried on directly between the housekeepers of these cities and the husbandmen who provisioned them from the nearby fields. The trading of the professional, on the other hand, is characterized by a different end, which is "profit". Considered in itself it has a certain debasement attaching to its activity, because it lacks "a virtuous or necessary end."

Since of itself it has no virtuous end, it must be directed to such an end; then it becomes lawful:

> Nothing prevents gain from being directed to some necessary or even virtuous end, and thus trading becomes lawful. Thus, for instance, a man may intend the moderate gain which he seeks to acquire by trading for the upkeep of his household, or for the assistance of the needy: or again, a man may take to trade for some public advantage, for instance lest his country lack the necessaries of life, and seek gain, not as an end, but as payment for his labour.[97]

cessariis ad vitam. Alia vero commutationis species est vel denariorum ad denarios, vel quarumcumque rerum ad denarios, non propter res necessarias vitae, sed propter lucrum quaerendum; et haec quidem negotiatio proprie videtur ad negotiatores pertinere, secundum Philosophum (*Polit.* lib. I, cap. 6). Prima autem commutatio laudabilis est, quia deservit naturali necessitati. Secunda autem juste vituperatur, quia, quantum est de se, deservit cupiditati lucri, quae terminum nescit, sed in infinitum tendit. Et ideo negotiatio secundum se considerata quamdam turpitudinem habet, inquantum non importat de sui ratione finem honestum vel necessarium.

[97]*S.T.*, IIa-IIae, q. 77, art. 4, c: Nihil prohibet lucrum ordinari ad aliquem finem necessarium vel etiam honestum; et sic negotiatio licita reddetur; sicut cum aliquis lucrum moderatum, quod negotiando quaerit, ordinat ad domus suae sustentationem, vel etiam ad sub-

Trading is lawful when it brings in needed provisions from other countries. It is also lawful when the merchant seeks a moderate gain "for the upkeep of the household." From this statement of Aquinas it is not to be understood, however, that merchants are justified in acting as middlemen between the city housekeeper and the nearby husbandmen, provided only that their gain be "for the upkeep of the household." Such an interpretation runs contrary to St. Thomas' contention (in the *De Regimine Principum* and in his *Commentary on the Politics)* that traders should be kept at a minimum. This is precisely why he urged the king to provision his city from its neighboring fields, in order that merchants might be dispensed with. They were to be tolerated only because they brought commodities from other countries. The 13th-century city ordinances that forbade the engrossing by merchants of foodstuffs within the territory surrounding the city, were in keeping with this teaching.[98] If the city is to be self-sufficient, and if, further, the number of its traders is to be kept at a minimum, then it will be necessary that a large number of its citizens, either living within its walls or within its trading territory, must practice husbandry. This number must be so proportioned to the total number of citizens that the town-country unit will be to a high degree self-sufficient. A widespread diffusion of husbandry is, therefore, necessary to keep in check the latent evils of trade.

5. The Rural Life and the Internal Peace of the State

Thus far it has been necessary to depend in large measure upon inference, in order to establish the proposi-

---

veniendum indigentibus; vel etiam cum aliquis negotiationi intendit propter publicam utiltatem, ne scilicet res necessariae ad vitam patriae desint; et lucrum expetit, non quasi finem, sed quasi stipendium laboris.

[98]Cf. *above*, chap. II, sect. 3.

tion that flourishing agrarian institutions are an essential part of Thomistic socio-economic order. That this inference is valid is borne out by certain explicit statements of Aquinas concerning an agrarian people. "That state," observes St. Thomas, "enjoys a greater measure of peace whose peoples are more sparsely assembled together and dwell in smaller proportion within the walls of the town."[99] And he agrees with Aristotle, that "it is more profitable to have the people engaged outside the cities, than for them to dwell constantly within the walls."[100] In this same truth he finds another argument against trade, for "if a city is given over to trade, it is of prime importance that the citizens be grouped in cities, and there engage in trade";[101] and when this happens the peace of the city will be endangered, "for when men are crowded together, it is an occasion of quarrels and all the elements for seditious plots are provided."[102] St. Thomas is aware that the conditions

---

[99]*The Governance of Rulers*, p. 118; *De Reg. Princ.*, II, 3: Civitas illa solet esse magis pacifica, cujus populus rarius congregatur, minusque intra urbis moenia resident.

[100]*Ibid.*: Unde secundum Aristotelis doctrinam, utilius est quidem quod populus extra civitates exerceatur, quam quod intra civitatis moenia jugiter commoretur.

[101]*Ibid.*: Si autem civitas sit mercationibus dedita, maxime necesse est intra urbem cives resideant, ibique mercationes exerceant.

[102]*The Governance of Rulers*, p. 118; *De Reg. Princ.*, II, 3: Ex frequenti enim hominum concursu datur occasio litibus, et seditionibus materia ministratur. A spurious part of the commentary on the *Politics—In Polit.*, VI. 4—offers a valuable commentary on this statement. The writer of this passage makes a good argument for his contention that an agricultural people is the best people. Lacking great riches, he observes, an agricultural people cannot readily leave their occupation outside of the city, where they are intent upon cultivating the land in order to secure the necessities of life. And so because they cannot leave these occupations removed from the city, they are not inclined to form gatherings in which they might plot evils. For men are wont, by reason of the mutual plotting that takes place in gatherings, to plan evil and to devise ways of rising against the rich and the rulers. For this reason they are better material

which foster class revolution or political anarchy are absent in a true agricultural people. An agrarian decentralized city-state holds in check man's tendencies toward social and economic disorder. Peace is the result of good order, and this is better secured in an agrarian people.

6. PROPERTY IN LAND AS THE BASIS OF SOCIAL ORDER

The ordered society, as St. Thomas conceived of it, was one in which men occupied a stable place in the social structure, and in which their activities were directed to some human need. The existence of such a society depended in large measure upon a strong agrarian domestic group, upon a well-organized agrarian occupational group, and, finally, upon the predominance of self-sufficient, independent town-country units. The existence and character of the domestic and occupational groups, in turn, was closely linked with the system of property in land prevailing at the time. The historical survey of the typical seigniory revealed that the character of this institution was determined by the system of property in land upon which it rested. This institution developed under a system in which the land was held, rather than owned absolutely: the lord held it under the king, and the dependent cultivators held it under the lord. Both lord and peasant were in stable possession of the land they cultivated. The lord enjoyed stability by reason of his authority; the peasant, in most instances at least, was guaranteed stable tenure through law and custom.[103] This stability insured a strong family life in the lord's household, and also in the peasant's; it allowed for cooperative agricul-

---

for citizenship (*ad politizandum*). Again, an agricultural people "is best because it is not covetous." It is less covetous of the riches and honors of others than is a people congregated within a city.

[103]Cf. *above*, chap. II, 2, c. When this stability was lost in the course of the sixteenth to the nineteenth centuries—the period of the evictions of the English peasants—great hardships followed.

ture on the seigniory and in the village; it allowed for an intricate three-field system of husbandry and for the use of communal lands.[104]

The system of ownership defended by Aquinas is that of private property.   He defends this institution as natural, being derived from the *jus gentium*.[105]   The private ownership defended by Aquinas is not, however, the absolute, socially irresponsible ownership that exists at the present. He defends a system of private ownership with community of use: .

> With St. Thomas, then, the principle of private ownership remains intact but the system which it generates must be so linked with social purpose and the common good as to be inseparable from them. . . The principle of distribution, or community of use, is a necessary corollary of the right of private ownership.[106]

The right of private ownership is valid as a means whereby a man may enjoy the peaceful use of some piece of property.   A man has the right, for example, to a particular field because he can make an opportune use of it.

> For if a particular piece of land be considered absolutely, it contains no reason why it should belong to one man more than to another, but if it be considered in respect to the opportunity for cultivation that it presents, and in respect to its unmolested use, then it has a certain commensuration to be the property of one and not of another

---

[104]Cf. *above*, chap. II, 2, g.

[105]Cf. McDonald, William J., *The Social Value of Property according to Saint Thomas Aquinas*, Washington, D.C.: Catholic University of America Press, 1939, pp. 90-6.

[106]McDonald, W. J., *op. cit.*, p. 95.

man, as the Philosopher shows *(Polit.,* II, 2).[107]

The lord of the seigniory had a right to the private ownership of land as a means for its peaceful cultivation.   But he
understood more clearly than does the modern landlord, that
his right was valid only as a means to his right of use, and
that the latter is a right common to all mankind, which
must be interpreted and exercised within such limits that
its realizaion would be possible for his fellowmen likewise.[108]
The lord only held the land under the king in trust, and was
obliged in social justice to respect the rights of the peasants
who, in turn, held and cultivated land under him.   Because
they were in a position opportunely to cultivate the plot of
land upon which they lived, they had a right to stable tenure
upon it, which custom forced the lord to respect.   In short,
the lord's ownership was interpreted in terms of the common good.

Again, St. Thomas' insistence that the system of private property respect the common good, insured for the
peasants a right in the waste lands.   These were of such a
nature that they were most opportunely used, when used in
common.   The lords were not permitted to approprite them
completely for themselves.   The same was true of the common use of stubble land in the three-field open system of
husbandry.   Because the people were accustomed to think
of a common use of private property, they were more ready
to cooperate in the common use of stubble land for grazing
purposes than would be true today when the notion of
community of use has been lost.

Further implications are entailed in the Thomistic

---

[107]*S.T.,* IIa-IIae, q. 57, art. 3, c: Si enim consideretur iste ager
absolute, non habet unde magis sit huius quam illius; sed se consideretur per respectum ad opportunitatem colendi, et ad pacificum usum
agri, secundum hoc habet quemdam commensurationem ad hoc quod
sit unius et non alterius, ut patet per Philosophum in *Polit.* II.

[108]Cf. Ryan, John A., *A Living Wage,* N. Y.: The Macmillan Co.,
1906, pp. 104-5.

teaching that the "principle of private ownership. . .must be
. . .linked with social purpose and the common good."[109]
Now it may be necessary for the common good that the sale
of private property be regulated.   Both Aristotle and
Aquinas defend those ancient precepts that regulate the
sale of possessions with a view to the common good of the
nation.   In his defense of the judicial precepts of the Old
Law, St. Thomas is confronted with the objection that, the
Old Law takes away the meaning of sale when it legislates
that a possession, alienated through sale, must be returned,
in the fiftieth year of the Jubilee, to the one who sold it.
Such a law, the objection continues, inasmuch as it weakens
the institution of buying and selling—an institution that
renders good service to society—is not fitting.[110]   In answer to this objection St. Thomas quotes Aristotle, and
affirms that the regulation of possessions is fitting, because
it is necessary for the common good of the city, or nation:

> As the Philosopher says *(Polit.* II.), the regu-
> lation of possessions conduces much to the preser-
> vation of a state or nation.   Consequently, as he
> himself observes, it was forbidden by the law in
> some of the heathen states, that anyone should
> sell his possessions, except to avoid a manifest loss.
> For if possessions were to be sold indiscriminately,
> they might happen to come into the hands of a
> few; so that it might become necessary for a state
> or country to become void of inhabitants.   Hence
> the Old Law, in order to remove this danger,
> ordered things in such a way that while provision
> was made for men's needs, by allowing the sale of

---

[109]McDonald, W. J., *op. cit.*, p. 95.

[110]Cf. *S.T.*, Ia-IIae, q. 105, art. 2, obj. 3: Societas hominum maxime conservatur per hoc quod homines emendo et vendendo sibi invicem res suas communicant, quibus indigent, ut dicitur (*Polit.*, lib.
1, cap. 5 et 7).   Sed lex vetus abstulit virtutem venditionis; mandavit
enim quod possessio vendita reverteretur ad venditorem in quinqua-
gesimo anno Jubilaei, ut patet (*Levit.* xxv).   Inconvenienter igitur
lex populum illum circa hoc instituit.

possessions to avail for a certain period, at the same time the said danger was removed, by prescribing the return of these possessions after that period had elapsed. The reason for this law was to prevent confusion of possessions, and to ensure the continuance of a definite distinction among the tribes.[111]

St. Thomas is here defending the propriety of a law that regulates the sale, not of any possessions whatsoever, but of possessions in land. The objection did not concern the sale in perpetuity, of city houses and of other mobile goods; for the Law permitted this. The number of these, Aquinas notes, is not fixed, but permits of addition.[112] To each of the tribes, on the contrary, was given a fixed amount of land, to which, in the nature of things, nothing could be added. For this reason it was fitting that the allotments of this land should be regulated. In this St. Thomas attests to the peculiar nature of property in land. The rights of private ownership of land are conditioned by the needs of the community.

---

[111]*S.T.*, Ia-IIae, q. 105, art. 2, ad 3: Sicut Philosophus dicit (*Polit.* lib. II, cap. 5), 'regulatio possessionum multum confert ad conservationem civitatis vel gentis.' Unde, sicut ipse dicit (*ibid.*), apud quasdam Gentilium civitates statutum fuit ut nullus possessionem vendere posset nisi pro manifesto detrimento. Si enim passim possessiones vendantur, potest contingere quod omnes possessiones ad paucos deveniant; et ita necesse erit civitatem vel regionem habitatoribus evacuari. Et ideo lex vetus ad hujusmodi periculum removendum sic ordinavit quod et necessitatibus hominum subveniretur, concedens possessionum venditionem usque ad certum tempus; et tamen periculum removit, praecipiens ut certo tempore possessio vendita ad vendentem rediret; et hoc instituit ut sortes non confunderentur, sed semper remaneret eadem distinctio determinata in tribubus.

[112]Cf. *S.T.*, Ia-IIae, q. 105, art. 2, ad 3: Quia vero domus urbanae non erant sorte distinctae, ideo concessit quod in perpetuum vendi possent, sicut et mobilia bona. Non enim erat statutus numerus domorum civitatis, sicut erat certa mensura possessionis, ad quam non addebatur. Poterat autem aliquid addi ad numerum domorum civitatis.

St. Thomas does not seem anywhere to have applied his general teaching on property in land to the seigniorial institution of his day. It may be that while rightly stressing religious and moral principles he did not always give sufficient attention to the social framework required for their implementation. Had he done so their significance would have been more apparent and their application to modern times facilitated. Having failed to do so it was necessary to adopt the more laborious method of inference, and in this way interpret principle in terms of the historical background. As a result of this process it is possible to state that the general principles St. Thomas lays down concerning private property favor the institution of the seigniory with its stability of land tenure; with its common use of waste lands and resources; and with its cooperative husbandry. The institution of private property, as he conceived of it, could be embodied in agrarian institutions other than the seigniory. But always the one condition of private ownership must be realized, namely, that this system be linked with the common good. That is to say, that the system be such as to allow for a sound agrarian domestic and occupational order within the state. Ultimately, it is the nature of the system of property in land that will determine whether or not good socio-economic order will prevail in the state.

The strongest justification for asserting that rural life plays an important rôle in the philosophy of St. Thomas, lies in the fact that a thriving rural life provides a foundation for the socio-economic order of the state. The rural people are an ordered people. They are ordered within the family group where they cooperate as parent or child, paterfamilias or servant, in securing the necessaries of life. The rural family is a true cell of society contributing with special effectiveness by the functions it performs to the life of the state. As members of the village group, the rural people cooperate in the common occupation of husbandry according to different levels of function. In this manner they form a true vocational group. Further, the wealth-getting activities of the rural people fall under the control of a natural teleology which checks man's propensities to greed. Production is directed to a definite goal: whether this be the necessaries of life for a particular household, or village, or city within some city-country unit. The rural people, to the extent that they produce for use, bring order to the economic life of the state, especially in that sphere pertaining to food, clothing and shelter. The problems of food distribution are much simplified among an agrarian people. St. Thomas favored a widespread diffusion of husbandry as a check upon trade in foodstuffs, and he favored rural life as better securing the peace of the state. A flourishing rural life is important in his philosophical synthesis because it is a condition for the good internal order of the state as he conceives of the latter.

CHAPTER V

THE IMPORTANCE OF THE PHILOSOPHICAL FACTOR IN THE DESTRUCTION OF MEDIEVAL AGRARIAN POLICY AND PRACTICE, WITH SPECIAL REFERENCE TO ENGLAND

Though speaking here of the destruction of medieval agrarian policy and practice, there is no intention to claim that all that was destroyed was good. Some of the aspects of medieval agrarian practice were clearly undesirable. Servile subjection, the tyranny of lords, the lack of sufficient incentives towards improved husbandry—these are difficult to defend in the old system. On the other hand, the good order of agrarian life based upon teleological considerations, the stability of land tenure, family security, cooperative husbandry in the seigniorial or village community, the protection of rights of tenure, the limitations of dues and rents through custom, and, finally, the natural curb upon greed—all these were worth bringing into the modern period. However, if it could be established that the retention of these undoubted socio-economic goods achieved by medieval agrarian policy and practices was inextricably bound up with the evils of that system, then it would be to no good purpose to speak of their dissolution. But this has not been established. For it is conceivable that the good characteristics of medieval agrarian practice might have been preserved while getting rid of the evil in that system. That this did not happen was due in no small measure to the advent of a new economic philosophy that brought about the destruction of the system before it could adjust itself to the needs and possibilities of a new age.

It is not easy to isolate the philosophical factor from the other causes that contributed to the destruction of medieval agrarian practice. However, the problem is much simplified by focusing our attention upon the agrarian changes and their causes as these took place in but one country. Only by restricting the problem in this manner will it be possible, within the limits of this chapter, to make a convincing case for the primacy of the philosophical factor in causing an agrarian revolution. The example of England offers itself as a convincing one for demonstrating this truth. Here the emphasis upon individual rights, which was of the essence of the growing Liberalistic thought in Western Europe from the 16th to the 19th centuries, redounded in a special way to the benefit of the lords, enabling them to escape their social responsibilities as holders of land. Medieval agrarian order had depended upon the acceptance of these responsibilities. Moreover, the English liberalistic conception of rights of property in land, if it did not cause the similar conception of property rights that came to prevail in America, was at least its prototype.

1. THE CHANGE IN AGRARIAN CONDITIONS

Some of the changes appearing in medieval agrarian conditions have already been considered in the historical section[1] of this study. There, mention was made of the change from services to rents in kind and rents in money, of the less favorable position of the lord of the seigniory with the advent of the money economy, and of the decrease in unfreedom within the villein classes. These changes do not, however, represent a destruction of medieval agrarian practice such as occurred from the 16th to the 19th centuries in England, and brought in their wake a social revolution. In this period, the one to which special attention will be given in this chapter, such factors as the enclosure movement, the destruction of the commons, the practice of

---

[1] Cf. *above*, chap. II.

farming out estates, the increase in fines levied upon the peasants entering upon a copyhold, and the conversion of copyholds into leases effected what may well be regarded as a revolutionary change in agrarian life.   Before going on to a description of these changes, it should be noted again that this examination of agrarian changes from the 16th to the 19th centuries and their causes is confined almost entirely to the English scene.   There is no intention to imply that the problem was exactly the same on the Continent.   The enclosure movement, for example, did not occur in France and Germany.[2]   In this chapter it is shown that a causal connection existed between the revolutionary changes in England and the growth there of a new philosophy hostile to the old agrarian order; and it is merely suggested that such a causal connection might be found in the other countries where the medieval agrarian order, very similar at one time to that in England, also gave way.

a) Enclosures and the Destruction of the Commons

When speaking of the enclosure movement it is necessary to distinguish between the enclosing as practiced by the small cultivators, and causing no harm, and the large-scale enclosing which had far-reaching effects.   The latter was

> carried out by great men, not by small.   It proceeds wholesale, not piecemeal.   It does not consist in many little cultivators rearranging their holdings by purchase, or sale, or agreement, but in one great proprietor or his agent consolidating small holdings into great estates.   The new arrangements are imposed rapidly and with a high hand from without.   They do not arise gradually

----

[2]Cf. Ashley, W. J., *Economic Organization of England*, N. Y.: Longmans Green, 1914, p. 58.

from within through the spontaneous development
of the peasants' needs and resources.[3]

In those many instances when the lord's demesne lay scattered in the open fields, his separated acre or half-acre strips
did not allow for grazing. "To be able to enclose spaces of
convenient size he must somehow," as Ashley explains it,
"get into his hands the adjacent strips of his tenants. For
this and other reasons, we find that enclosure very commonly meant, in practice, the disappearance of a number of customary holdings in the open fields."[4] The process of enclosing was motivated by the "increased profitableness of
pasture farming, consequent upon the development of the
textile industries." It resulted in the multiplication of the
insecure, propertyless man.[5] The evil of the enclosure
movement did not extend itself to France and Germany.[6]

The cooperative use of the commons by the peasants
has already been explained in an earlier chapter.[7] According to Tawney this was a very important part of medieval
agriculture:

> Commons and common rights, so far from be-
> ing merely a luxury or a convenience, were really
> an integral and indispensable part of the system
> of agriculture, a linch pin, the removal of which
> brought the whole structure of village society tum-
> bling down.[8]

The need of the small peasant for rights in the commons
went beyond the requirement for grazing land for his cattle

---

[3]Tawney, R. H., *The Agrarian Problem in the Sixteenth Century*,
N. Y.: Longmans Green, 1912, p. 180.

[4]Ashley, W. J., *Economic Organization of England*, N. Y.: Longmans Green, 1914, pp. 57-8.

[5]Tawney, R. H., *op. cit.*, pp. 195, 280.

[6]Cf. Ashley, W. J., *op. cit.*, p. 58.

[7]Cf. *above*, chap. II, 2, g.

[8]Tawney, R. H., *op. cit.*, pp. 238-9.

and sheep. He needed plough beasts for the cultivation of his arable land; these he could not keep without grazing rights in the commons. When he was deprived of the latter, then all his husbandry was threatened. The monopolizing of commons by manorial authorities was achieved in several stages. First they usually began by overstocking the common pasture, with the consequent edging out of the small man. Later, after much friction, enclosure followed as a way of regularizing the new arrangements.[9]

b) *Means Used in Forcing Peasants from Their Holdings*

The extreme lucrativeness of sheep-farming, and the depreciation in the value of money, offered an incentive to the landlords to make the most profitable use which they could of their property by amalgating small holdings into large leasehold farms,[10] which were used mainly, though not entirely for pasture. To do this, as was pointed out above, they had to get rid of the small tenants. When the tenants held their land at the will of the lord, or if their leases were for a short term of years, in both instances the lords could get rid of them quite easily by simply revoking the lease at will, or at the end of the short term. But where the tenants

---

[9]Cf. Tawney, R. H., *op. cit.*, pp. 242-3.

[10]Ashley, W. J., *The Economic Organization of England*, p. 54, offers an explanation for the derivation of "farmer." "A fixed payment in lieu of varying receipts or profits was known in the middle ages as a 'ferm' (Latin: firma); and the lessee of a demesne for a term of years was accordingly, known as a 'firmar', 'fermor', or 'farmer'. In the fifteenth and sixteenth centuries we may say with some confidence that 'farmer', when used in an agricultural sense, most commonly meant a person who had taken on lease a demesne or part of a demesne; it was much later that it was extended to include every person in charge, on his own account, of an agricultural 'holding'." Ashley also states, *op. cit.*, p. 65, that this system of farming out land led to the growth of the competitive spirit.

were copyholders[11] with the estate of inheritance, the lords had only two alternatives—to induce them to accept leases,[12] or to raise the fines for admission, payable by those who had the inherited right to hold land on the manor. As a consequence the tenants had to surrender their holdings or pay the full competitive entry price to keep them. The result was an "almost revolutionary deterioration in their position."[13] Custom was no longer strong enough to protect them:

> Hitherto the custom of the manor had been a dyke which protected them against the downward pressure of competition, and behind which they built up their prosperity. Now the unearned increment was transferred from tenant to landlord by the simple process of capitalizing it in the fine demanded on entry.[14]

These agrarian changes of the 16th century continued through the subsequent centuries into the 19th. What

---

[11]The copyholder was a tenant 'by copy of court roll according to the custom of the manor', and possesses his title in his own keeping. Cf. Tawney, R. H., *op. cit.*, p. 47.

[12]Ashley, W. J., *op. cit.*, p. 131-4, writing of the change effected in the legal status of many peasants during the 16th century states that "they had been induced to 'surrender their copies,' which so long as they retained them might perhaps have given them a secure heritable estate, in return for leases for lives or for terms of years." The effect of the change from copyhold into leasehold, when there was no express right of renewal, had a far reaching effect: "it turned the landlord into the absolute owner, with a legal right to dispose of the land as he pleased, instead of being a partial owner only, sharing the property in it with a tenant who enjoyed an heritable right—in other words, it destroyed the semi-proprietorship of the peasant copyholder."

[13]Tawney, R. H., *op. cit.*, p. 310.

[14]Tawney, R. H., *op. cit.*, p. 310. Cf. also p. 407: "The tenure of the vast majority of small cultivators left them free to be squeezed out by exorbitant fines, and to be evicted when the lives for which most of them held their copies came to an end."

has been said of these early stages of the agrarian changes
is generally applicable to the latter. Thus, the enclosure
movement was by no means completed in the 16th century,
during which it had affected only certain districts in
England. It continued into the 18th and 19th centuries
when, according to Ashley, it went forward "with fresh
ardour; and between 1760 and 1850, by means of Enclosure
Acts, practically all the remaining open fields and most of
the commons were swept away."[15] The motive remained
generally the same—the opportunity to supply a needed
product with gain. In Tudor times it was the demand for
wool; in the later period, it was the high price of wheat
which occasioned this opportunity. A growth in extension
of landed estates, and the intensification of the landlord's
ownership within the several manors went on "briskly during the first three-quarters of the eighteenth century." So
also with the amalgamation of farms. In the last half of
the 18th century a policy was carried out whereby the small
plots of the poor were laid to the great farms.[16]

2. Non-philosophical Factors

It is not to be denied that other factors, besides the
philosophical, were partially instrumental in effecting these
changes in agrarian policy and practice. These should not,
however, be over emphasized. Thus, for example, a gradual evolution of agricultural techniques occurred between
the medieval and the modern period, and this somewhat influenced agrarian practices. However, changes in agricultural technique "do not by themselves account for the special social consequences which flowed from the agrarian
changes of the sixteenth century."[17] Again, the far-reach-

---

[15]Ashley, W. J., *op. cit.*, p. 137.
[16]Cf. Ashley, W. J., *The Economic Organization of England*, pp.
131, 134, 137.
[17]Tawney, R. H., *op. cit.*, p. 406.

ing effects of the Black Death, or the Great Plague, as it is sometimes called, upon agrarian conditions, are not to be overlooked. But here also Tawney warns against generalization:

> The more fully manorial records are explored, the more difficult does it seem to generalize about the effects of that great catastrophe. One cannot say that it was the beginning of the commutation of labour services into rents, for on some manors they were partially commuted before it, and on some they were not entirely commuted till nearly two centuries later. One cannot say that the leasing of the demesne was due to the Plague; for where the labour supply was small, parts of it were leased already, and after the Plague the authorities of different manors met the crisis in different ways, sometimes beginning by letting the demesne only to return later to the older system.[18]

What is more certainly true, is that the Great Plague, which decreased the number of available cultivators, merely accelerated such significant tendencies as the leasing of the lord's demesne, and the sale of land, tendencies that already existed before this catastrophe.[19] Finally, the enclosures are not to be regarded as an inevitable consequence of the growth of the textile industry. As Tawney points out,

> Many customary tenants practiced sheep-farming upon a considerable scale, and it is not easy to discover any economic reason why the cheap wool required for the development of the cloth-manufacturing industry should not have been supplied by the very peasants in whose cottages it was carded and spun and woven.[20]

[18]Tawney, R. H., *op. cit.,* p. 90.

[19]Cf. *Ibid.;* also Ashley, W. J., *Economic Organization of England,* p. 49, who states that the commutation of labor services for money payments was common before the Plague.

[20]Tawney, R. H., *op. cit.,* p. 407.

Tawney concludes that the economic factor does not explain the devastating agrarian changes that took place after the medieval period.

> We cannot therefore agree with those writers who regard the decline in the position of the smaller landed classes, which took place in our period (16th century), as an inevitable step in economic progress, similar to the decay of one type of industry before the competition of another. If economic causes made a new system of farming profitable, it is none the less true that legal causes decided by whom the profits should be enjoyed.[21]

The question involved in the 16th-century agrarian revolution was rather one of land tenure than of agricultural technique:

> Men do not only leave the land; they are forced off it. Not only economic, but legal, issues are involved, and the latter give a decisive twist to the former. What made the new methods of agriculture not simply an important technical advance in the utilization of the soil, but the beginning of a social revolution, was the insecurity of the tenure of large numbers of the peasantry, in the absence of which they might gradually have adapted themselves to the altered conditions, without any overwhelming shock to the rural life such as was produced by the evictions and by the loss of rights of common.[22]

Up to the time of this social revolution the peasant's tenure of land was secured through custom and law. The latter received their inspiration and force from a socio-economic philosophy that interpreted property rights in terms of the

---

[21]*Ibid.*

[22]Tawney, R. H., *op. cit.,* p. 406.

common good.[23]   This condition no longer obtained in the
16th and subsequent centuries when a new philosophy had
changed men's outlook.

3. THE PHILOSOPHICAL FACTOR

a) The New Mechanistic Conception of Society

The conception of the agrarian domestic and occupational order, as it was outlined in the preceding chapter, is
teleological.   The end or function is, in every case, the ultimate determinant of order within the various individual
social groups, as it is the determinant of the general ordering of all the social groups to each other and to the State;
and likewise, it is the end that measures and regulates the
different social or economic functions, such as wealth-getting, within the social body.   This teleological conception
"had been the keystone holding together the social fabric."[24]
This conception of society gradually gave way to one that
was mechanistic.

It will not be possible within the limits of this study to
consider all the teachings and influences that entered into
the formation of this new conception of society.   Attention
will be confined mainly to the 18th-century contributions of
the Physiocrats in France and of Adam Smith in England,
in whose writings the new liberalistic and mechanistic
philosophy received clear expression.   These writers were
the heirs of a liberalistic philosophy that was already in the
ascendancy during the centuries that preceded the 18th, and
during which there was a gradual transition of thought
from the medieval conception of society to the new
mechanistic outlook.

---

[23]Cf. *above*, chap. IV, sect. 6.

[24]Tawney, R. H., *The Acquisitive Society*, N. Y.: Harcourt, Brace,
1920, p. 12.

On the authority of Max Weber and Professor Tawney, Laski asserts that the rise of Protestantism aided the growth of this liberal philosophy[25] which came gradually to win concessions from religion. According to Tawney the most important concession won was the understanding that religion is to restrict its activities to the regulation of the individual's relation with God; and that it was to claim no authority to interfere with man's social relations and activities.[26] Religious authority, which had in the past insisted that attention be given to moral considerations in economic planning, was now discredited in the business world. Forgetting that man was a social and political being, this school of thought would limit the realm of religion to the individual's relation with God.

The streams of thought that entered into the formation of the new liberalism were various. During the 16th and 17th centuries there arose a new scientific outlook that is reflected later in the thought of the Physiocrats. With Machiavelli, who expressed the spirit of the Renaissance, there is a new lust for power, an admiration for power, a

---

[25]Cf. Laski, H., *The Rise of Liberalism*, p. 23.

[26]Cf. Tawney, R. H., *Religion and the Rise of Capitalism*, N. Y.: Harcourt, Brace, 1926, pp. 279, 6-13, 177-93; Fanfani, A., *Catholicism, Protestantism and Capitalism*, N. Y.: Sheed and Ward, 1939, who finds that the pre-capitalistic spirit of the 13th century gradually gave way to the capitalistic spirit in the course of the period from the 14th to the 16th century inclusive, when Europe was still largely Catholic. He writes, "it is the waning of faith that explains the establishment of a capitalistic spirit in a Catholic world." p. 178. On the other hand, he also finds that Protestantism gave an impetus to the formation of the capitalistic spirit. "Protestantism," he writes, "encouraged capitalism inasmuch as it denied the relation between earthly action and eternal recompense." p. 205; Weber, Max, *The Protestant Ethic and the Spirit of Capitalism*, London: George Allen and Unwin, 1930, attributes to the Protestant ethic the growth of an economic system that he calls Rationalism. By this he means a system based not on custom or tradition, but on the deliberate and systematic adjustment of economic means to the attainment of the objective of pecuniary profit.

carelessness of means, a rejection of medieval bonds, and a frank paganism.[27] The political theory of Bodin advocated the absolute supremacy of the State.[27a] Mercantilism, that whole body of state economic policy which developed in Western Europe during the 15th to the 17th centuries, gave the control of economic life to the State and for the State. This transfer of social control from the Church to the State in the economic realm was momentous. With it there took place a shift of goals for economic activity. In the words of Laski, "the motive of state action is no longer the good life, but the attainment of wealth, the enactment, by legislation, of the conditions that will make for wealth."[28] During the 16th century many of the ideas that will form the liberalistic and mechanistic outlook of Adam Smith and the Physiocrats in the 18th century have already come to be accepted.

b) Physical Interpretation of the Natural Law; Individualism

The mechanistic conception of society rested upon a physical interpretation of the natural law, developed by the Physiocrats.[29] This group taught that men "are subject to natural laws[30] in the same way that the equilibrium of

---

[27]Cf. Laski, H., *The Rise of Liberalism*, p. 39.

[27a]Cf. Laski, H., *op. cit.*, p. 43.

[28]Laski, H., *op. cit.*, p. 59.

[29]This school, flourishing in France in the 18th century, was so denominated from the word *physeikratia*, meaning nature's rule. Cf. Beer, M., *An Inquiry into Physiocracy*, London: George Allen and Unwin, 1939, p. 148.

[30]St. Thomas would not speak of the "natural laws" as in the plural. In his teaching, the natural law is a participation of the eternal law in the rational creature, by which the latter is inclined to his proper act and goal. Cf. *S.T.*, Ia-IIae, q. 91, art. 2, c; and which governs him that he may live according to the order of his own reason, to the order of the higher human authority, and to the order of the Divine Law. Cf. *S.T.*, Ia-IIae, q. 87, art. 1, c. This conception of the natural law is obviously not at all like that of the Physiocrats.

nature is maintained by physical laws."[31]   Quesnay
(1694-1774), a leading figure of this school, held that nature
should be allowed to rule according to the inherent laws
given to it by Providence.   Max Beer writes that

> he had also learned from the physical interpreta-
> tion of the law of nature that self-interest could
> not be suppressed, since the physical laws—accord-
> ing to the light of the new physical science—
> necessarily operated in a causative sequence.[32]

Quesnay argued from this necessary character of the law of
nature to the removal of economic restraints:

> It was therefore best to allow nature and
> right reason to work in liberty, to remove all those
> commercial regulations which give to one of the
> parties an advantage over the other.   The empha-
> sis on liberty or free competition as the best—
> because natural—regulator of prices, is the only
> factor which could reform medieval society into a
> *royaume agricole* as Quesnay visualized it.[33]

Quesnay proclaimed this emphasis upon liberty, or free
competition, in his well-known *"laisser passer, laisser
faire."*[34]   He expresses the same teaching when he writes,
"pas trop gouverner! Ne tentez pas fixer les prix. La
concurrence seule peut regler les prix avec équité."[35]

The Physiocrats had developed the doctrine of self-

---

[31]Haney, Lewis H., *History of Economic Thought*, N. Y.: Macmillan, 1924, p. 166.

[32]Beer, M., *An Inquiry into Physiocracy*, London: George Allen
and Unwin, 1939, p. 148.   Cf. also Haney, L. H., *op. cit.*, p. 165, who
quotes the same teaching of the Physiocrat, Mercier de la Riviére
from his *L'Ordre Naturel*.

[33]*Ibid.*

[34]Quesnay, F., *Oeuvres Economiques et Philosophiques*, ed. Au-
guste Oncken, Frankfort: Baer, 1888, p. 671.

[35]Quesnay, F., *Oeuvres*, p. 804.

interest principally in favor of the landlords of France. With Adam Smith the same doctrine is urged in behalf of the merchants.[36] In opposition to the oft-repeated teaching of Aquinas and Aristotle that, unless the seeking of wealth is controlled by some fixed end or purpose, it will go on to infinity, Adam Smith sought to demonstrate that men should be left unhindered in their pursuit of wealth. By attending to their wants men will automatically promote the social good, even though they may be acting from a motive that is purely selfish. Consequently, Adam Smith argues, all economic restraints such as those on trade should be removed:

> Every individual is continually exerting himself to find out the most advantageous employment for whatever capital he can command. It is his own advantage, indeed, and not that of the society, which he has in view. But the study of his own advantage naturally, or rather necessarily leads him to prefer that employment which is most advantageous to the society.[37]

Such a conception of society is clearly mechanistic.[38] There is no purposeful ordering of individual wealth-getting

---

[36]Laski, H., *The Rise of Liberalism*, N. Y.: Harpers, 1936, p. 211.

[37]Adam Smith, *An Inquiry into the Nature and Causes of the Wealth of Nations*, Cannan ed., N. Y.: Random House, (Modern Library), 1937, p. 421; Cf. also p. 423: The individual "intends only his own security, and by directing that industry in such a manner a· its produce may be of the greatest value, he intends only his own gain, and he is in this, as in many other cases, led by an invisible hand to promote an end which was no part of his intention."

[38]Cf. Tawney, R. H., *Religion and the Rise of Capitalism*, p. 191, has described its mechanistic character very well. It rests on a "social philosophy which repudiated teleology, and which substituted the analogy of a self-regulating mechanism, moved by the weights and pulleys of economic motives for the theory which had regarded society as an organism composed of different classes united by their common subordination to a spiritual purpose." Cf. also Tawney, R. H., *The Acquisitive Society*, N. Y.: Harcourt, Brace, 1920, p. 16.

to a common end or goal. The latter is achieved necessarily, mechanically, so long as each strives selfishly and
independently to produce wealth in the manner, and to the
amount that he conceives to be most desirable. Whatever
cooperation is exercised towards a common end is exerted
blindly. Laski's interesting commentary on this doctrine
of simple liberty is to the point.

> For Adam Smith the myriad spontaneous
> actions of individuals, made for their own private
> benefit, result by a mysterious alchemy, in social
> good. We do better for society by this 'simple
> system of natural liberty' than if we consciously
> contrived its advantage. Underlying the structure
> of the universe is sympathy which compels the
> good of others to be involved in my good. . .If man
> is left alone, he will work out his own salvation.
> Whatever disturbs the order of nature makes for
> evil and not for benefit.[39]

If, then, this pursuit of wealth for its own sake is by its
very nature ordered to the common good, then the government will exist, not to coordinate individual wealth-getting
to the common good, but rather to guarantee security for
the enlightened and free enterprise of the individuals.

This new economic philosophy created a society in
which individualism could flourish, without much hindrance,
and with little, if any, sense of guilt. Obviously, in such a
society, the group spirit and the association tendencies that
had prevailed on the seigniory and in the rural village
community would be destroyed. The seigniory and the
village community could flourish only where there was a
recognition of a common end, and where there was an
acceptance, by all the members of the community, of those

---

[39]Laski, H., *The Rise of Liberalism, the Philosophy of a Business
Civilization*, N. Y.: Harper, 1936, pp. 200-1. Cf. also p. 205, where
he remarks that "with Adam Smith the business man is given his
letters of credit."

restrictions upon their individual liberty that might be entailed in the joint furtherance of this end. The members
of the community were prompted by a sense of social justice
to recognize the right of everyone to enough land to secure
at least his basic necessities. Their cooperative organization of medieval rural life was such that most men were
satisfied when they had acquired an amount of wealth sufficient for the needs of the household. For, before the new
philosophy had taken hold of men's minds, they were
generally inclined towards viewing wealth-getting in terms
of purpose. What they knew to be true in theory, namely,
that wealth-getting is a means, not an end, their institutions helped them to live up to in practice.

With the advent of the individualistic conception of
society, there came an inclination to make wealth-getting
an end in itself. To do this was to encourage man's latent
greed—unnatural concupiscence, as Aquinas calls it—for
the infinite. Once the *laissez faire* principle was admitted,
there was little to prevent a man from the selfish pursuit
of wealth, with its consequent disruption of the balanced,
teleological organization of the village community, upon
which group security had depended. If such a man wished
to justify his action he could do so on the grounds that it
would necessarily lead to the wider common good of the
whole nation, even though it accomplished this at the
expense of the local common good. The effect of his individualism would be cumulative. The greed of this one man,
inasmuch as it was a threat to the security of others, caused
them, in turn, to become greedy to compensate by individual
security for that which they had lost in collective security.
Men were less inclined to be satisfied with subsistence husbandry, and sought to be farmers for profit. The restraints
of seigniorial or village community life, such as labor services, dues in kind or in money, a limited acreage, regulated
crops—all were incompatible with the new spirit and the
new goal, the pursuit of wealth for its own sake. Under
the onslaught of this individualism, medieval agrarian life

was not given a fair chance to adjust itself to the circumstances of post-renaissance life, before it was destroyed. Of this *laissez faire* spirit and its power to transform agrarian conditions, Tawney writes:

> But if the intoxication with dreams of boundless material possibilities, the divorce of economic from moral considerations, the restless experiment and initiative and contempt for restrictions that fetter them, which are the marks of that spirit's operations, are never quite so victorious in agriculture as they are in finance, it is nevertheless in transforming agrarian conditions that its nature and characteristics are most impressively revealed.[40]

Not only was this individualistic spirit a determining factor in changing the agrarian conditions of the 16th century, the period for which Tawney writes, but it also exerted great influence upon the 18th and 19th-century changes, through the writings of the later liberalists such as Adam Smith. Economic individualism existed from the 16th century on, and during all this period it gradually destroyed the medieval agrarian life which had been organized on a social basis. As one writer, speaking for the 17th century puts it, "the group spirit and association tendencies that had prevailed so long, gave way, in the seventeenth century, to individualism—'individualism of mind and soul and purse'."[41]

c) The Individualistic Concept of Private Property in Land

In all the important agrarian changes of our period the issue of property in land was involved. The movement of

---

[40]Tawney, R. H., *The Agrarian Problem in the Sixteenth Century*, p. 408.

[41]Czajkowski, Casimer J., *Theory of Private Property in John Locke's Political Philosophy*, dissert., Notre Dame University, 1941, p. 15.

enclosures, the disregard of the peasant's rights in the commons, the conversion of copyhold tenure into tenure by lease, the increase in entry fines and rents—all these changes were resisted by the peasants on the basis of their property rights. For centuries the small cultivators, whether free or unfree, had enjoyed stability of tenure. When this stability of tenure was threatened, many had no higher court of appeal than the custom of the seigniory, or manor, which had formerly given them security. In the 16th century, under the impact of the liberalistic philosophy and the new economic conditions, the protecting dyke of custom gave way, and those institutions which had depended upon the stability of tenure, heretofore guaranteed by custom, were destroyed. According to Tawney it was this breakdown that made the agrarian changes revolutionary.[42] Had there been a power to insist that the small cultivators' rights over the land they possessed were quite as inviolable as the rights later claimed by the landlords, then the new found freedom to pursue wealth for its own sake would have been resisted at the outset by the inertia of the old agrarian institutions. Since this was not the case, the institutions gave way along with the customary right of tenure.

Though St. Thomas defends a system of private ownership, he does not however justify absolute, socially irresponsible ownership. He defends a system of private ownership with community of use. The system of private ownership must be "linked with social purpose and the common good."[43] As long as this concept of property in land dominated men's minds, so long law and custom were able to insure stability of tenure to the small cultivator. The new liberalistic philosophy, with its emphasis upon individual enterprise and upon efficiency in the pursuit of

---

[42]Cf. Tawney, R. H., *The Agrarian Problem in the Sixteenth Century*, pp. 407-8.

[43]Cf. *above*, chap. IV, sect. 6.

wealth, in effect rejected the Thomistic concept of private ownership with community of use.

The writings of John Locke were very influential in encouraging an individualistic concept of property. It is by labor that rights over things are gained. In the words of Locke, "it is the labour then which puts the greatest part of the value upon the land, without which it would scarcely be worth anything."[44] The laborer's right to property is limited by the rights of others to the same. Locke places a second limitation upon this right. "One may not appropriate by his labor more than he can 'use to any advantage of life before it spoils'."[45] The same limitation is placed upon the amount of land that one may appropriate by his labor. Only as much land "as a man tills, plants, improves, cultivates, and can use the product of, so much is his property."[46] However, Locke offers a convenient means of evading this second limitation. As Larkin points out, "thanks to the 'invention of money, and the tacit agreement of men to put a value on it', one may lawfully acquire an indefinite number of things by his labour. Money, being a store of value and a medium of exchange, prevents things from perishing."[47] By this tacit agreement in regard to money men have in effect "agreed to a disproportionate and unequal possession of the earth."[48]

Locke's furtherance of an individualistic conception of private property is due to this emphasis upon the individual's right, as against the state's. As a consequence, "the duties of property and the responsibilities of ownership

---

[44]Locke, John, *Two Treatises of Civil Government*, in general works, London, 1824, Vol. 4, bk. II, chap. 5, no. 43.

[45]Larkin, Pascal, *Property in the Eighteenth Century, with special reference to England and Locke*, Cork: Cork University Press, 1930, p. 63, quoting Locke, J., *Two Treatises of Civil Government*, bk. II, chap. 5, no. 31.

[46]Locke, J., *op. cit.*, bk. II, chap. 5, no. 32.

[47]Larkin, P., *op. cit.*, p. 63.

[48]Locke, J., *op. cit.*, bk. II, chap. 5, no. 50.

were thus thrust into the background."[49] Moreover, his treatment of property was only incidental to his treatment of the problems of civil government, and "his theory, in itself, is not nearly so important as the effects it produced amongst a wide circle of admirers in England, France and the early American colonies."[50]

The Physiocrats held an absolutistic view of property somewhat like Locke's,[51] although Max Beer affirms that Quesnay's view is not entirely absolutistic.[52] It was in the general spirit of the philosophy of the Physiocrats to protect the landlords.[53] In keeping with his doctrine of self-interest, Adam Smith believed that the individual should be given "the greatest possible measure of freedom in the use and disposal of his property."[54] The interest of the landlords he thought to be "strictly and inseparably connected with the general interest of the society."[55] His approach to the question of rents is arithmetical. With a rise in prices of agricultural products there will be a rise in rents, with the latter rising faster than the former.

> The rise in the price of cattle, for example, tends too to raise the rent of land directly, and in a still greater proportion. The real value of the landlord's share, his real command of the labour of other people, not only rises with the real value of the produce, but the proportion of his share to the whole produce rises with it. That produce,

---

[49]Larkin, P., *op. cit.*, p. 79.

[50]McDonald, W. J., *The Social Value of Property according to St. Thomas Aquinas*, p. 104.

[51]*Ibid.*

[52]Beer, Max, *An Inquiry into Physiocracy*, London: George Allen and Unwin, 1939, p. 112.

[53]Cf. Quesnay, F., *Oeuvres*, p. 331.

[54]McDonald, *op. cit.*, p. 106.

[55]Adam Smith, *The Wealth of Nations*, Cannon ed., pp. 248-9.

after the rise in its real price, requires no more labour to collect it than before.[56]

After a careful study of property in the eighteenth century Larkin concludes that by the end of that century the "conception of private property as an absolute individual right had triumphed."[57] This conception of property that "triumphed" in the eighteenth century was taking hold of men's minds even in the sixteenth century when liberalism was already in the ascendancy. This change in men's thinking on property created an alien atmosphere in which the custom of the manor could not survive. The custom protecting the property rights of the small cultivator could exert a force only so long as it reflected a social concept of property in men's minds. Once it was accepted that property rights are absolute, then it was inevitable that the landlords, moved by the pursuit of wealth for its own sake, should use their land in complete disregard of the rights of the dependent cultivators. The result was the serious breakdown in agrarian institutions from the sixteenth to the nineteenth centuries.

d) *Influences Helping to Shape the Early Theories on Property in Land in America*

The influence of Locke is evident in the social history of America since the Revolution. This is the opinion of Larkin who writes that "Locke's individualism, his glorification of property rights and his love of commerce have been interwoven into the economic and social texture of Ameri-

---

[56]Adam Smith, *op. cit.*, pp. 247-8; In regard to this teaching of Smith, Larkin, *op. cit.*, p. 95, offers the explanation that the landlords' title to income rested "on their active participation in the production of wealth or in the performance of some public service." This was more true in Smith's time and in medieval times than it is today.

[57]Larkin, P., *op. cit.*, p. 135.

can life."[58] Locke's teaching influenced such important leaders as Paine, John Adams, Clinton, and Madison.

Harrington, in his *Oceana,* published in London in 1656, had advocated a wide distribution of property for social welfare. James Otis, who came under his influence in America, recognized the responsibilities entailed in ownership, but, unfortunately, was not given a great hearing. "In his *Rights of Colonies,* Otis opposed the Lockian system at many points and is more in line with the older tradition. But his ideas were washed aside in the flow of events."[59]

It is quite impossible to ascertain the elements that entered into the formation of Thomas Jefferson's thought on private property. Undoubtedly, much of it was original.[60] However, he was influenced somewhat by the Lockian individualism.[61] He shared with the Physiocrats their strong leaning toward agriculture. Theoretically, at least, he was convinced that prominence should be given to agriculture, and he was convinced that the United States would always be essentially an agricultural nation.[62] History has shown that America did not remain an essentially agricultural nation, certainly not in the sense that it remained a nation wherein there was a wide distribution of property in land.

In America, as in England and France, ownership came to be a legal, rather than a social or

---

[58]Larkin, P., *op. cit.*, p. 171. In remarking upon this coincidence of Lockian and American thought, Larkin does not intend to judge to what extent there existed a causal connection between the two. Cf. p. 172.

[59]McDonald, *op. cit.*, p. 109.

[60]Cf. *Correspondence of Jefferson and Du Pont de Nemours,* ed. Chinard, G., Baltimore: Johns Hopkins Press, 1931, p. XII; Larkin, P., *op. cit.*, p. 158.

[61]Cf. Larkin, P., *op. cit.*, p. 148.

[62]Cf. Chinard, G., *op. cit.*, pp. XII, XLVII, LI.

ethical, matter. It was gradually given over to
the will of the State and under benign government-
al patronage the race for wealth and power was
carried on apace. Instead of the former wide distribution of property a condition arose in which a
comparatively small number controlled the means
of distribution and the vast majority became wage
slaves. Ownership was no longer a general feature
of society determining its character.[63]

e) Conclusion

The influence of the philosophical factor in the destruction of the old agrarian order has been viewed under two
general aspects: first, in so far as it encouraged individualism in the pursuit of wealth, and secondly, in so far as it
removed the barriers to such a pursuit of wealth by justify-
ing the individual in the unhampered acquisition and disposal of property in land. With the destruction of the old
agrarian institutions a new society came into existence, one
to which might appropriately be given the name of the
Acquisitive Society, a name by which Professor Tawney has
described our contemporary order. The Acquisitive
Society, according to Tawney, is one whose "whole tendency
and interest and preoccupation is to promote the acquisition
of wealth."[64] It is a society that protects this right of
pursuing wealth, with little, if any, regard that this right
correspond to the fulfillment of a needed function.[65] It is
a society that, by recognizing the pursuit of riches as an
end, offers the "enchanting vision of infinite expansion,"[66]
a vision from which Aristotle and St. Thomas had sought
to protect the weak eyes of man. It is a society that stands
in contrast to the Functional Society, "which aimed at mak-

---

[63]McDonald, *op. cit.*, pp. 110-111.
[64]Tawney, R. H., *The Acquisitive Society*, p. 29.
[65]Cf. Tawney, R. H., *op. cit.*, p. 30.
[66]*Ibid.*

ing the acquisition of wealth contingent upon the discharge of social obligations, which sought to proportion remuneration to service and denied it to those by whom no service was performed."[67]   It is not hard to see that the way to the Acquisitive Society was prepared by the philosophy of economic liberalism.   Admittedly, the medieval agrarian institutions were not perfect representations of the functional order.   But they were approximations.   Had they been allowed to grow in the intellectual and moral atmosphere created by a teleological economic philosophy, it is quite conceivable that they would have come to embody a true functional order to an ever higher degree.

---

[67]Tawney, R. H., *op. cit.*, pp. 28-9.

CHAPTER VI

AN AGRARIAN POLICY CONSISTENT WITH THOMISTIC PRINCIPLES

1. THE LAND AND PERSONAL VALUES

"The scope of every social life remains identical, sacred, obligatory: it is the development of the personal values of man as the image of God."[1] All political, social, and economic planning is ordained that man may attain the destiny suitable to his nature. Man is the image of God by reason of his intellectual nature,[2] and his highest values will be those of intellect and will. All other values, such as those in which the body participates, take their meaning from the former. A wise agrarian policy must therefore seek to bring to men all values, and in due order.

In a similar vein of thought St. Thomas writes that the ultimate purpose of society is to bring men through virtuous living to the possession of God.[3] Among all the moral virtues, the virtue of religion, by which we bind ourselves to God as to an unfailing principle,[4] is preeminent.[5] The

---

[1]Pius XII, "1942 Christmas Message," in *Catholic Mind*, Vol. XLI, no. 961, Jan., 1943, pp. 49-50. Cf. also p. 48; and *S.T.*, Ia-IIae, q. 92, art. 1, c; and Briefs, G., *The Proletariat*, p. 269.

[2]Cf. *S.T.*, Ia, q. 93, art. 2, c: Solae intellectuales creaturae, proprie loquendo, sunt ad imaginem Dei.

[3]Cf. *above*, chap. III, introduction; and *De Reg. Princ.*, I, 14.

[4]Cf. *S.T.*, IIa-IIae, q. 81, art. 1, c: Religio proprie importat ordinem ad Deum. Ipse enim est cui principaliter alligari debemus tamquam indeficienti principio.

[5]Cf. *S.T.*, IIa-IIae, q. 81, art. 6, c: Religio praeeminet inter alias virtutes morales.

rural environment and the occupation of husbandry, as these were analyzed in an earlier chapter on agriculture and personal values,[6] are of themselves apt for the practice of religion.   The life of the husbandman is one of close cooperation with, and constant dependence upon, God.   Unless he deliberately blind himself to the supernatural which presses upon him in his working environment, it will be natural to the husbandman to recognize God as the Lord of all creation, and thence to bind himself to Him through the virtue of religion.   The occupation of husbandry inasmuch as it allows for the balanced development of man, for this reason also prepares him for the practice of the virtue of religion.   Not only is rural life of itself suitable to man's personal religious development, but the stability of rural institutions—the family and the community—that will come with a sound agrarian policy, will also favor the development of religious institutions and corporate worship.[7]

In this age of a great multiplication of material goods it becomes ever more evident that man has failed to realize many of the values by which he should live—even such as are material.   A large section of our population is without that sufficiency of bodily goods—food, clothing—necessary for the practice of virtue.[8]   Many people, both urban and rural, are forced to live in an environment where a decent standard of living is impossible.

More alarming than the failure of man to achieve, in this age of technical progress, a decent material standard of living, is his failure to attain the higher values perfecting his soul.   Such is the misfortune of a vast number

---

[6] Cf. *above*, chap. III.

[7] Cf. Agar, Herbert, *Land of the Free*, p. 37, who believes it to be well proven that giant cosmopolitan cities are unfriendly to the practice of the virtue of religion.

[8] Cf. Agar, Herbert, *Land of the Free*, Boston: Houghton Mifflin, 1935, p. 43, reporting the findings of the Brooking's Institute; Schmiedeler, Edgar, *Balanced Abundance*, N.C.W.C. pamphlet, N. Y.: Paulist Press, 1937, pp. 4-5.

among the propertyless workers who live in spiritual poverty. It is of these that Pius XI speaks with deep regret.

> How universally has the true Christian spirit become impaired which formerly produced such lofty sentiments even in uncultured and illiterate men! In its stead, man's one solicitude is to obtain his daily bread in any way he can. And so bodily labor, which was decreed by Providence for the good of man's body and soul even after original sin, has everywhere been changed into an instrument of strange perversion: for dead matter leaves the factory ennobled and transformed, where men are corrupted and degraded.[9]

a) Contemporary Conditions of Labor

Without attempting a full analysis of the causes underlying this impairing of the Christian spirit, this failure of man to advance in spiritual things, one cause—the one singled out by the Pope—may certainly be assigned for this evil. The working man's spiritual life has been stunted because manual labor instead of perfecting him as a man, as it can do when it is performed in keeping with the standards set by St. Thomas for such labor,[10] has dehumanized him. The Pope has clearly implied that formerly a causal connection existed between manual labor and the formation of a true Christian spirit.[11] This is no longer true today

---

[9]Pius XI, encyclical letter, *Quadragesimo Anno*, N. Y.: The America Press, 1938, p. 38.

[10]Cf. *above*, chap. III.

[11]Cf. also Pius XII, *Quoniam Paschalia Sollemnia*, April 9, 1939, in *Principles for Peace*, n. 1318: "For work is not only, for every man, a means of decent livelihood, but it is the means through which all those manifold powers and faculties with which nature, training and art have endowed the dignity of the human personality, find their necessary expression, and this with a certain comeliness."

when manual labor has become "an instrument of strange perversion." This condemnation is leveled at factory labor which, as has been pointed out in an earlier chapter,[12] often compels man to work with but a few of his many faculties. Modern laboring conditions, with all that this implies—the lack of ownership of productive property, and the nature of the work itself—have been instrumental in forming a proletarian class,[13] which includes also a "huge army of rural wage workers."[14] Manual labor on the land has not deserved nor received such terrible condemnation from the Pope.

b) A Use of the Machine That Will Allow for More Leisurely Living on the Land

The machine which should "better the personal condition of the worker,"[15] and which should lighten his efforts to attain the necessities of life, is not yet being used to best advantage. The emphasis in farm machinery, to take an example relevant to the present study, has been upon large

---

[12]Cf. *above*, chap. III.

[13]Briefs, G. A., *The Proletariat*, N. Y.: McGraw-Hill, 1937, p. 50, has defined a proletarian as "a propertyless wage earner (representative of the great mass of such created by the capitalistic order) who regards himself and kind as constituting a distinct social class, who lives and forms his ideas in the light of this class consciousness according to class ideals, and who on the basis of this class consciousness rejects the prevailing social and economic order." Cf. p. 40, *circa*, where he offers as an explanation for the growth of the proletarian class that a man who in factory work does not find the experiences that will uphold his sense of dignity and worth, will seek it in mass (proletarian) action; also Schmiedeler, Edgar, *Our Rural Proletariat*, N.C.W.C. pamphlet, N.Y.: Paulist Press, 1938; and Ligutti and Rawe, *Rural Roads to Security*, Milwaukee: Bruce, 1940, p. 32.

[14]Pius XI, encyclical letter, *Quadragesimo Anno*, in *Principles for Peace*, n. 976.

[15]Pius XII, *Pentecostal Address on Labor*, June 13, 1943.

units that make possible the cultivation of large tracts of land with little man-power, thus "freeing" many men for other forms of production. Though the large machine has saved man-power, it has not made for leisurely living. With the multiplication of the large farm machine men have been displaced from the land. Those remaining must work as hard as before—perhaps more so—to compensate for the loss of man-power, to realize a return on the capital they have invested in machinery and to meet the extensive charges of highly mechanized farming. This precludes the possibility of much leisure in their lives. Nor will those displaced experience more leisure. They will become engaged mainly in manufacturing, in the service industries, and in clerical work. Much of what they produce will undoubtedly be necessary that society may have a reasonably high standard of living. Yet the likelihood exists that in our acquisitive society, where "all economic activity is equally estimable, whether it is subordinated to a social purpose or not,"[16] that some of their human energy will be wasted on the production of unneeded luxuries or services, simply because men will be found willing and able to pay for them. In any event, our present economy demands that they be somehow employed and producing. What has therefore been effected by our large agricultural machinery, and non-agricultural also, is more production but not more leisure in working.[17]

Certain advantages would result from an emphasis upon small machines[18] designed not so much to increase the total production per man-power unit operating on the land,

---

[16]Tawney, R. H., *The Acquisitive Society*, N. Y.: Harcourt, Brace, 1920, p. 33; cf. also *below*, sect. on "Production for Use."

[17]It will be noted that in this section "leisure in working" has been taken as distinguished from leisure or free time after working hours. The forty hour week gives much of this latter, but it also creates the problem of leisure time.

[18]Cf. Penty, A. J., *op. cit.*, p. 94, who finds the issue in the problems caused by machines to be between large and small machines.

but rather to lighten the toil involved in the production of agricultural products. Such a policy will encourage farming on a smaller scale, such as on the family-size farm, or the part-time farm. Inasmuch as the need of any one family, or community or city-country unit for agricultural products is fixed within certain general limits, a use of small labor-saving machines could reasonably be expected to give these social groups more leisure for cultural pursuits, taking the latter phrase in its widest connotation.[19] Whatever policy is adopted in regard to farm machinery, it must take into account the exigencies of a sound agrarian order in which human values are most completely realized. It may not force the order to conform itself to the requirements of mechanical efficiency. Thus the very large farm cannot be justified merely on the ground that it is a condition for the profitable use of the large machine.

c) Urbanization

Connected with the contemporary poverty of spiritual values is the present trend toward urbanization. This social phenomenon has often in the past "brought decay in the fibre of a people. . . No civilization survives when the urbanite becomes the model for all groups."[20] In the recent past urban civilization had only been "a comparatively light superstructure which rested on the broad and solid foundations of rural society." But today, when the shift of population—due to a one-sided emphasis upon scientific, mechan-

---

[19]Man's increased control over his environment has not resulted in the formation of an integral culture. Modern mass culture has in fact threatened man's personality. Cf. Dawson, C., *Judgment of the Nations*, N. Y.: Sheed and Ward, 1942, pp. 117, 125, 126; Sorokin, Pitirim A., *The Crisis of Our Age*, N. Y.: Dutton, 1941, pp. 16-7.

[20]Hocking, W. E., "A Philosophy of Life for the American Farmer (and others)," in *1940 Agricultural Yearbook*, Washington: Government Printing Office, 1940, p. 1066.

ical, and industrial progress—has gone so far in favor of the city, the superstructure is no longer light nor the foundation solid.   The present civilization that has lost its agrarian moorings stands in danger.[21]

It has not proved to be a civilization in which the best in man has been brought to the fore. No one policy or course of action can bring this ideal about. But, among other steps to be taken, it is imperative that the dignity of manual labor be restored. Until ways can be found to radically improve industrial working conditions through such reforms as the restoration of productive property in industry to the many, until that time more men should be helped to an occupation on the land—full-time or part-time. If human values are primary, then the laboring man may not be sacrificed no matter what the material end is in view. But the restoration of dignity to labor is not alone sufficient to bring man to a fuller life.   Over and above this, he must also be integrated into society through family life, community life; and his life must be carried out on a more functional basis.[22]   It is to this end that the agrarian policy outlined in the following sections of this chapter is directed.

2. REESTABLISHING A STRONG DOMESTIC ORDER UPON THE LAND

a) Land and the Family

In his *Pentecostal Address* of 1941, Pope Pius XII writes that "it is in the spirit of *Rerum Novarum* to state that, as a rule, only that stability which is rooted in one's

---

[21]Dawson, C., *Progress and Religion*, London: Sheed and Ward, 1933, pp. 211-15.

[22]Briefs, G., *op. cit.*, p. 284, believes that Western civilization will be in grave danger until this is done.

own holding,[23] makes of the family the vital and most perfect and fecund cell of society."[24]   In like manner, it is in the spirit of St. Thomas' philosophy to state that a strong domestic order in the nation will not be realized unless the family be well founded upon the land.   The domestic order, as Aquinas conceived of it,[25] comprised in itself the relations of husband to wife, father to son, and master to servant. The manager of the household was to be guided by the virtue of *oeconomica,* to which, in turn, the art of wealth-getting was subservient.   Viewed against the background of Aquinas' time, the domestic rule was far from a mere formality.   The rule of the paterfamilias was exercised throughout the day; it extended beyond his authority over wife and children, to the servants and to the dependent cultivators; it practiced the virtue of *oeconomica* in directing the use of natural wealth to the good life; it directed the art of wealth-getting, with all the manifold seigniorial activities that this involved; it was an orderly rule with a real relation to the orderly rule of the city-state.   Christopher Dawson calls attention to the significant role of the family, so conceived, in its relation to the good order of the state: "thus the base of the social edifice was constituted by the family as the primary social and economic unity.   Beneath and upholding politics—the Law of the city—there was economics—the Law of the household."[26]

The existence of human society generally demands private property; but it is demanded in a special way by the

---

[23]In context, "holding" is a holding of land; it is private property in land; it is vital space for the family.

[24]Pius XII, *La Solennita della Pentecoste,* commemorating the Fiftieth Anniversary of the encyclical *Rerum Novarum* of Pope Leo XIII, June 1, 1941, in *Principles for Peace,* ed. Koenig, H. C., Washington: N.C.W.C., 1943, n. 1692.

[25]Cf. chap. IV, sect. 2, on the Rural Domestic Group.

[26]Dawson, Christopher, *Judgment of the Nations,* N.Y.: Sheed and Ward, 1942, p. 189.

exigencies of the family. Pius XII, commenting upon the *Rerum Novarum*, writes as follows:

> According to the teaching of *Rerum Novarum*, nature itself has closely joined private property with the existence of human society and its true civilization, and in a very special manner with the existence and development of the family.[27]

Private property is requisite for the father of a family that he may secure "the healthy liberty he needs in order to fulfill the duties assigned him by the Creator regarding the physical, spiritual, and religious welfare of the family."[28] Having stated the family's need for private property in general, the Pope next states that the land is, in a special way, the object of private property. The land is of special import to the family which will be able to draw from it its subsistence.

> Of all the goods that can be the object of private property, none is more conformable to nature, according to the teaching of *Rerum Novarum*, than the land, the holding on which the family lives, and from the products of which it draws all or part of its subsistence.[29]

Private property in land will give the family a stability that will make it "the vital and most perfect and fecund cell of society, joining up in a brilliant manner in its progressive cohesion the present and future generations."[30] The Pope regards it as imperative that the family be given *Lebensraum*. The family that is prevented, by conditions over which it has no power, from securing a homestead, is, as it

---

[27] Pius XII, *La Solennita della Pentecoste*, in *Principles for Peace*, n. 1691.

[28] *Ibid.*

[29] Pius XII, *op. cit.*, n. 1692.

[30] *Ibid.*

were, in "fetters"; it cannot carry out its proper functions.[31]

It is a cardinal tenet of the National Catholic Rural Life Conference, that "the farm is the native habitat of the family."[32] Agricultural society, in contrast to "industrial society which works against the family and in favor of divorce, desertion, temporary unions, companionate marriage . . . is characterized by the strength, permanence, and unity of the marriage bond and the comparative rarity of its dissolution."[33] Where "the occupational and the social activities of city life tend to develop an individualism which destroys the unity of family life . . . the occupation of agri-

---

[31]Cf. Pius XII, *op. cit.*, n. 1692. The Pope's statement, in the form of a question, points unmistakably to the need of land for the family: "if today the concept and the creation of vital spaces is at the center of social and political aims, should not one, before all else, think of the vital space of the family and free it of the fetters of conditions which do not permit one even to formulate the idea of a homestead of one's own?" The same idea is expressed in the Christmas message of 1942, op. cit., n. 1848: "he should give to the family —that unique cell of the people—space, light and air so that it may attend to its mission. . .and that it may preserve, fortify and reconstitute, according to its powers, its proper economic, spiritual, moral and juridic unity."

[32]*Manifesto on Rural Life*, National Catholic Rural Life Conference, Milwaukee: Bruce, 1939, p. 3.

[33]Evidence is not wanting that an industrial society, as the *Manifesto*, pp. 3-4, points out, works against the strong family unit. In the U. S. there were 164 divorces per 1000 marriages in 1935. Cf. Leclercq, J., and Hanley, T. R., *Marriage and the Family*, N. Y.: Pustet, 1941, p. 168. It is hardly necessary to give figures for the drop in the contemporary birth rate. As a result of the lowering birth rate the median age of the population in the U. S. increased from 26.4 years in 1930 to 28.9 years in 1940. Leclercq foresees a large decline in the native population of the Western world. He writes: "unless a recovery, no signs whereof are so far visible takes place, all the countries of Western Europe as well as the United States will witness in the second half of the present century a shrinkage of their native population in a proportion varying between a quarter and a half." *op. cit.*, pp. 238-9. This represents a serious threat to our civilization. *op. cit.*, pp. 238-9, *passim*.

culture. . . by its very nature tends to promote the unity of family life and to strengthen the marriage bond."[34] The family should be helped towards becoming a unit of production, that it may be less dependent upon outside agencies for the basic necessities of life. The reestablishment of families on family-size farms offers a means of avoiding the problem of mal-distributed overproduction and a means of directing production to the immediate need of the home.[35] Such a policy is, moreover, in accord with economic efficiency.[36]

---

[34]*Manifesto*, pp. 3-4, *passim*. In our non-farm population, the production of foodstuffs, the processing of food, and even the immediate preparation of food, are becoming ever more divorced from normal family functioning. There remain scarcely enough functions to call for any family organization whatsoever. The contribution of these cells to society is negligible; instead of supporting the institutions of society, they have come to depend upon them. Cf. Baker, O. E., *Address given at N. C. State College of Agriculture and Engineering*, Aug. 4, 1938. Washington: Bureau of Agricultural Economics, 1939, p. 4, for the positive correlation between good diet and home-produced food.

[35]*Manifesto*, p. 13.

[36]Cf. Ryan, John A., *A Better Economic Order*, N.Y.: Harper, 1935, p. 154, who believes a great extension of small farm units to be an economic requisite for agriculture. "In the vast majority of cases," he writes, "the farm that can be cultivated by one family seems to be the most profitable." On the other hand, O'Brien, George, "Some Lessons for Irish Agriculture From Western Europe," in *Studies*, Irish Quarterly, Vol. 29: 367-81, warns that a low standard of living will result when farms become too small. Abraham Lincoln stated in his "Milwaukee Address on Agriculture," in *Washington, Jefferson, Lincoln, and Agriculture*, Washington: Bureau of Agricultural Economics, 1937, p. 87, that "ere long the most valuable of all arts, will be the art of deriving a comfortable subsistence from the smallest area of soil." The School of Living, Suffern, N.Y., has very carefully worked out a series of "How to Economize" bulletins, the purpose of which is to show that, from the purely economic motive of financial saving, the home can well afford to spend time in producing or processing foods. These bulletins offer a strong economic argument for a greater family self-sufficiency.

The strength of the domestic order upon the land is revealed in the contribution it makes toward the maintenance and increase of population, a problem that must be faced today. While urban families are perishing, the rural families persist. "The modern urban philosophy of life," according to one authority, "apparently, tends toward extinction; the rural philosophy of life tends toward survival."[37] Accordingly, there must be a reemphasis upon a familistic economic system[38] resting upon agriculture. The present trends revealed by statistical studies "indicate that in some way more families must be raised in a rural environment, where conditions are more favorable to family life than in our large cities, if a decline in population, and very probably in cvilization, is to be avoided."[39]

---

[37]Baker, O. E., Borsodi, R., Wilson, M. L., *Agriculture in Modern Life*, N.Y.: Harper, 1939, Part I, "Our Rural People," by O. E. Baker, p. 38. Cf. also, Bureau of the Census, Special Report, "The Net Reproduction Rate," from *Dynamic America*, Apr. 1941: "The urban areas had a net reproduction rate of only 76 in 1940...The rural-nonfarm population had a net reproduction rate of 116 in 1940...The rural-farm population had the highest net reproduction rate of all three residence areas, 136 in 1940."

[38]Dr. Baker, *op. cit.*, pp. 6-7, recognizes five major economic systems—the familistic, the individualistic, the capitalistic, the cooperative, and the socialistic. He describes the familistic system as one "that generally tends toward the widespread ownership of property and the increase of population, indeed, commonly leads toward a population so dense as to lower the standards of living...The system is associated with love of the land and family loyalty. The family is the economic as well as the social unit." Cf. also Baker, O. E., *Circular 300*, Bureau of Agricultural Economics, p. 9; and Taylor, Carl C., *Rural Sociology*, N. Y., Harper, 1933, p. 271.

[39]Baker, Borsodi, Wilson, *op. cit.*, pp. 9-10. Dr. Baker proposes not a complete return to a rural-familistic economy but a better balance between the five economic systems that will permit participation in the benefits of each.

b) *The Weakened Rural Family in the United States*

The trend of events during the last decades has not been toward reestablishing the family on the land. The new possibilities of greater food production with less man-power afforded by modern invention, and the modern tendency—a reflection of the acquisitive spirit—to emphasize production for sale and profit rather than for use, have caused the growth of large farms, often at the expense of the family-size farms. According to the 1940 census this growth has been considerable.[40] Of those families that are on the land, many are insecure and without the resources in good land, in sufficient land, and in capital to enjoy flourishing family life. The President's Committee on Farm Tenancy finds a "series of groups of farm families whose insecurity is a threat to the integrity of rural life. The families comprised within these groups constitute fully half the total farm population of the country."[41]

Instability and insecurity of farm families, in the words of the Committee, "leach the binding elements of rural community life." Such family groups cannot support

---

[40]A meager 1.6 percent of the farmers of the nation—those farming 1000 acres or more—now operate 34.3 per cent of all land in farms. Farms of 10,000 acres and over account for 14 per cent of all land farmed in the U. S. Cf. Schmiedeler, Edgar, *Vanishing Homesteads*, N.C.W.C. pamphlet, N.Y.: Paulist Press, 1941, p. 11.

[41]*Farm Tenancy, Report of the President's Committee*, February, 1937, Washington: U. S. Government Printing Office, p. 4. Among the insecure groups are the tenants, the croppers, the farm laborers, the families on submarginal land, the families on holdings of inadequate size, the owner families hopelessly in debt, and the farm young people unable to obtain farms. pp. 4-5. The security of tenure under the seigniorial system is better appreciated when it is compared with the lot of the farm tenants of the U. S. in 1935. More than a third (34.2 percent) of the 2,865,000 tenant farmers of the nation had been occupying their farms only one year in the spring of 1935. p. 5. Adding to this rural insecurity is the increasing number of farm laborers who migrate both as individuals and as families. These work mainly on intensive (commercial) crops. pp. 4-5.

the social edifice. The strong rural family was traditional in America.[42] Its contribution as a true and fecund cell of society has been great. It must be preserved and multiplied as a means of giving vitality and stability to the life of the nation: "the Nation must put large numbers of farm families into a relationship to the land adequate for their self-support."[43]

c) Part-time Farming

Modern transportation facilities have made it possible for the family to live on the land, even when its head is not engaged in full-time farming, but is employed elsewhere. This subsistence, or part-time farming, has much to recommend it; it preserves the values of family life upon the land while at the same time providing labor for the manufacture of those things that will raise the general standard of living. By providing an opportunity for creative work on the land it offsets the dehumanizing effects of mechanical, repetitious factory work. This way of life has already been sanctioned by practice in this country. A program of subsistence farming will enable the city or town to attain, in a greater measure, to that self-sufficiency in food, advocated by St. Thomas for the city-country unit.

d) The Multi-family Farm

The Thomistic concept of the family, a concept wider than that of the family today,[44] was reflected in the organization of the seigniory, or manor. The authority of the paterfamilias extended not merely to the household servants, but also went out to those dependent cultivators who, while they owed him services, yet enjoyed their own family life upon the land. This arrangement had its good points:

---

[42]Cf. Agar, Herbert, *Land of the Free*, Boston: Houghton Mifflin, 1935, pp. 38-40, *passim*; *Farm Tenancy Report*, pp. 3, 6.

[43]*Farm Tenancy Report*, p. 7.

[44]Cf. *above*, chap. IV, sect. 2.

it answered the lord's need for laborers; it gave family life, stable tenure, direction, and at least a limited·freedom to the laborers. It was a presupposition of this system that the great accidental differences among·men warrant an arrangement in which the more capable will lead the less capable to their good. Undoubtedly, this arrangement led to great abuses. But this is not sufficient reason for rejecting it in its entirety. These same great accidental differences exist between men today. Consequently a policy will be in error if it overstresses the equality among men to the point of rejecting all hierarchical organization in society.[45]

An agrarian policy that would seek for anything like mathematical equality in the distribution of land to families would not be in accord with this Thomistic principle of a hierarchical organization of society, nor would it be in accord with man's nature. Today, as in the past, men differ widely in their capabilities. Some will show a greater capability for using large tracts of land effectively.[46] That one man should be farming a large tract of land, does not in itself represent a social·evil. However in these cases the governing principle must be that the large owner recognize the demands of the common good in the use of the

---

[45]Cf. Pius XI, encyclical *Divini Redemptoris*, 1937, in *Principles for Peace*, n. 1202-6, for his condemnation of "a pseudo-ideal of justice of equality and fraternity in labor" such as is proclaimed by Atheistic Communism. Of the Communist's rejection of all hierarchy in the organization of society, the Pope writes: "in man's relations with other individuals, besides, Communists hold the principle of absolute equality, rejecting all hierarchy and divinely-constituted authority, including the authority of parents." n. 1204. In the Letter of Cardinal Maglione, Secretary of State, to La Semaine Sociale de France meeting in Bordeaux, *Documentation Catholique*, 1939, in *Principles for Peace*, n. 1359, the recognition of classes in society is shown to be a condition for social order; cf. Tawney, R. H., *Equality*, London: Allen and Unwin, 1938, p. 39.

[46]Cf. *Farm Tenancy, Report of President's Committee*, Washington: U. S. Government Printing Office, 1937, p. 13. "Families vary greatly in their capacity for independent management."

land he holds. His ownership should not prevent others from establishing homes on the land. The large owner would, for example, be meeting this demand if he gave to those laboring on his fields the opportunity of gradually acquiring ownership of a family-size, or subsistence, plot within the limits of his estate. Such an arrangement would make provision for that class of men who cannot attain full ownership independently, and who perhaps would find themselves unable to retain ownership after they had attained it. This might be due to their lack of capital, or industry, or even desire for private ownership of land. It is better for the improvident, and more conducive to the common good, that they should participate in the domestic order of the larger owner, rather than to be thrown upon the State. Any such policy allowing for the formation of farm units containing within them dependent family groups, must be framed with great care lest the evils of the medieval seigniory or the old estate system in this country should again come to the fore. On the other hand, to deny altogether the possibility of a domestic order in which the more capable and enterprising man will be given the opportunity of bringing order among a number of families, who are in a limited way dependent upon him, would seem to be a waste of administrative talent. As Aquinas observed, it would be unfitting that the superior person should not use his talents for the benefit of others.[47]

3. THE RURAL COMMUNITY

a) Occupational Organization Within the Rural Community

In his classic work on the *Reorganization of the Social Economy*, Nell-Breuning[48] points out that atomist-individualist thought has destroyed all smaller communities

---

[47]Cf. *S.T.*, Ia, q. 96, art. 4, c.

[48]Nell-Breuning, Oswald Von, S. J., *Reorganization of the Social Economy*, transl. Dempsey, B. W., S. J., Milwaukee: Bruce, 1936.

of life, threatening even the family. As a result the State is confronted with a great emptiness. The community, the county, the guild, and numerous corporations and societies, had enriched the State. Without them society became a shapeless, unformed, monotonous mass, and thus the State was forced to strong measures to give it some semblance of form.[49] These observations echo the teaching of Aquinas that the "multitude (state) would not be ordered, but confused, if there were not in it different orders."[50] In this confusion the State is constrained to step in and to perform functions hat could be performed more efficiently by smaller and lower groups. This, according to Pius XI, is "a disturbance of right order." It is against the principle of Subsidiarity.[51] This analysis is applicable in some measure to the contemporary federal government of this country which finds itself constrained to enact social legislation in an attempt to remedy the lack of the nation's internal unity.

St. Thomas states that if confusion is to be avoided in the state then there must be a diversity of orders arising "from the diversity of offices and actions."[52] An occupational ordering of society is demanded by this explicit statement of Aquinas, by the general principles of his philosophy read in the light of their historical background, and by the example that he gives of these orders, namely, the order of "of those who labor in the fields."[53]

In calling for an occupational (vocational) organization of society, Pius XI, therefore, reflects the thought of St. Thomas. The Pope writes that "the aim of social legislation must therefore be the re-establishment of vocational

---

[49]Nell-Breuning. *op. cit.*, pp. 202-3.

[50]*S.T.*. Ia, q. 108, art. 2, c. Cf. *above*, chap. IV, sect. 3.

[51]Pius XI. *Quadragesimo Anno*, in Nell-Breuning, *op cit.*, par. 79-80.

[52]*S.T.*, Ia. q. 108, art. 2, c. Cf. *above*, chap. IV, sect. 3.

[53]*Ibid.*

groups."[54] These groups are formed by reason of occupational homogeneity, this being the *ratio* of its order. Within any group there will be those who direct and those who carry out the activity. This is the element of diversity. The group will be united by its common goal and by the complementary functioning of its members moving towards this goal.[55] The occupational group therefore represents a vertical division of society including those members of different ranks—orders[56]—who are united by a common occupation. The farm group is one of the vocational groups.[57]

In addition to the unity that they possess by reason of their vocational homogeneity, the members of the rural community are further united, as a municipality, by their neighborly homogeneity, to use a phrase of Nell-Breuning, who writes,

> Both the union of people based upon neighborly homogeneity and that based upon vocational homo-

---

[54]Pius XI, *op. cit.*, par. 82. Cf. also, Parson, Wilfrid, S. J., "What are Vocational Groups?", in *Thought*, Vol. 17, no. 66, Sept. '42.

[55]Nell-Breuning, *op. cit.*, pp. 220-222.

[56]"Order" taken concretely as those of one rank, who function at one level of activity. Cf. *above*, chap. IV, sect. 3.

[57]Nell-Breuning, *op. cit.*, p. 229. A complete plan for the vocational organization of agriculture would need to take into consideration the nationwide activities of all farmers. The present treatment will touch upon the problem only in connection with the rural community. Attention is called to the article of Dr. Schmiedeler, O.S.B., "Pius XI's New Social Order and Agriculture", in *Ecclesiastical Review*, October, 1940, where the interesting viewpoint is expressed that the policy of the AAA represented a beginning in the vocational organization of agriculture on a national basis. The AAA, he writes, "faced with the alternatives of handling all matters of policy and administration through a horde of government agents and calling upon the farmers themselves to participate actively in shaping policies of administering programs...chose the latter way." Cf. also, McShane, James, S. J., "Economic Democracy Through V-Groups," *Social Justice Review*, Vol. 36, nos. 6, 7, 8, 9, October to January, 1943-44, especially no. 9, making application to agriculture.

geneity appear natural to the Pope: 'These groups, in a true sense autonomous, are considered by many to be, if not essential to civil society, at least its natural and spontaneous development.'[58]

It is highly desirable from the viewpoint of the internal order of the State that the rural community should be strengthened.

In this connection the village community of medieval times, with its use of common land and its intricate manner of cooperation in production, deserves careful consideration. A modern adaptation of the village community idea should be fostered today. This is not to be understood as the mere transplanting of the village community unchanged from medieval to contemporary times; such a venture would be doomed to failure. For new factors, such as the predominance of the money economy, and the scientific and technological advances in agricultural production must be taken into account. These factors have created new problems in procuring and maintaining ownership of land; and in the production and marketing of agricultural products.

b) Cooperative Enterprise on a Community Basis

Cooperative enterprise may be used profitably as a means of adapting the medieval village idea to modern conditions. Thus, cooperatives have made it possible for the farmers of a community to unite in capitalizing their agricultural enterprises, such as the purchasing of costly farm machinery;[59] and to unite in the purchase and maintenance

---

[58]Nell-Breuning, *op. cit.*, p. 222, quoting *Quadragesimo Anno*, par. 83.

[59]Cf. Schmiedeler, Edgar, O.S.B., *Cooperation, a Christian Mode of Industry*, Ozone Park, N.Y.: Catholic Literary Guild, 1941, pp. 106-7, who describes the successful cooperative formed by the 25 Colorado farmers, for the purpose of buying harvesting machinery. In this instance the Farm Security Administration made the loan to the 25 as individuals. This is the multiborrowers type of loan.

of common land, which may again become necessary under the pressure of a greater population. Cooperatives enable them to join in the processing, standardization, and marketing of their products, and to form consumer's groups with which to supply those things in which they cannot easily, as individual families, be self-sufficient.[60]

Cooperatives, thus employed in connection with the rural community, are performing functions of a true vocational group.

> The farmer. . . should unite with fellow farmers in vocational groups. Although cooperatives may not realize completely the ideal of vocational grouping the Holy Father has in mind, they contain in their fundamental principles the possibilities for vocational organization.[61]

The common goal of the group is the production, processing, and distribution of food. By their joint action the members further this end more efficiently than they could as individuals. As a group they are able to determine reasonable standards of quality for their products and the just price; and for the same reason they have a better control upon the market.

The community cooperative that allows all to have a personal relation to the common good is a functional society.[62] A cooperative that ceases to be a functional society is without its *raison d'etre*, since cooperatives were first organized in order to oppose the acquisitive spirit. The organization of a cooperative to serve the rural community is both conducive to its proper functioning and to the adaptation of the community to modern conditions. A

---

[60]Cf. *Farm Tenancy*, p. 13, on rural cooperative enterprise.

[61]*Manifesto*, National Catholic Rural Life Conference, p. 56.

[62]Tawney, R. H., *The Acquisitive Society*, p. 180, lists as one of the conditions of a Functional Society, "that the producers shall stand in a direct relation to the community for whom production is carried on, so that their responsibility to it may be obvious and unmistakable."

great leader of the cooperative movement in this country, James Warbasse, stressed the possibility of this union. His suggestions are very much in keeping with St. Thomas' philosophy of self-sufficiency. Attributing the failure of certain cooperatives operating in farm colonies to the fact that they were on a producer basis—a profit business basis —he advocates production for use, rather than for sale. This he calls the consumer cooperative method, and sees in it a means of community self-sufficiency:

> The consumer cooperative method could now be applied to agriculture and could save this great industry. . . A colony or association of people on the land can organize as cooperative consumers and produce for themselves. They can make the home and the community nearly self-sufficient.[63]

The consumer cooperative can bring to the community "the wealth of inventions, mechanical devices, and the . . . resources of science."[64] The extent of self-sufficiency that is now possible for the rural community by reason of such factors as the distribution of electrical power into the countryside, and the facility of transportation, goes far beyond that envisioned by St. Thomas. Judged by the criterion of self-sufficiency, which for Aquinas was a mark of perfection in anything, the modern community is potentially more perfect and makes more adequate provision for the good life than its medieval counterpart.

4. A Greater Measure of Self-sufficiency for the City-Country Unit

For reasons that have already been studied in an earlier chapter,[65] St. Thomas advocated self-sufficiency in

---

[63]Warbasse, James Peter, "Cooperative Decentralization," in the *Decentralist*, Organ of the School of Living, Suffern, N. Y., Autumn, 1943, p. 10.

[64]Warbasse, J. P., *op. cit.*, p. 11.

[65]Cf. *above*, chap. IV, sect. 4.

foodstuffs for the city. He was aware, however, that in the nature of things the city would need some traders, but cautioned that it should make only a moderate use of them. Difficult as it is, in view of the modern facility in transporting goods, to interpret this principle for the modern city, the principle still appears to remain valid for the contemporary age.

In the foregoing discussion it was shown that a certain measure of self-sufficiency was desirable for the rural family and the rural community. Nature has given to these groups a certain autonomy, that must be realized if they are to remain strong, and are to contribute by their functioning to the good order of the state.

a) Excessive Dependence of the Contemporary Large City upon Outside Supplies

The large city of today is far from being self-sufficient through the foodstuffs that are supplied from its neighboring fields. In fact it is hardly conceivable that, with its present concentration of population in small areas, it could be self-sufficient. The modern economic system, with its complicated machinery of transportation and distribution has made the insufficiency of the large city appear a normal state of affairs. Modern transportation has undoubtedly given a new significance to the phrase, "the surrounding fields" of a city. It makes the produce of every field in the nation—and perhaps, in the world—available to the city. In the face of these facts it is nothing less than a radical departure to suggest that the modern city should seek for a certain measure of self-sufficiency.

St. Thomas rested his argument for self-sufficiency mainly upon the fact that the city would need to choose between being provisioned by its neighboring fields, or by many traders. He rejected the latter alternative because it brought disorder into the economic and social life of the city, by placing an unnatural emphasis upon wealth-getting for its own sake.[66]   The modern city, confronted with the same alternatives, has chosen the one rejected by St. Thomas.   The economic system that keeps the city supplied, rests upon great capital charges, transportation charges, charges of middlemen— in short upon the activity of many "traders," with attendant complication of, and a certain disorder in, economic and social life.

Certain courses of action are open to the modern city whereby it can keep in moderation the wide range of business activity by which it is provisioned.   Modern transportation has favored the development of part-time or subsistence farming, through which the city worker can secure part of his sustenance directly from the soil.[67]   A multiplication of subsistence family units will mean a great reduction in the traffic of foodstuffs that the city will need to carry on.[68]   Again, cooperative enterprise among the members of a city-country unit offers a means of provisioning the city with a minimum of profiteering.   To achieve this end, the cooperative production of food is joined under one management with its cooperative distribution and consumption.[69]   Where this condition obtains, the conflict of interests between producers and consumers is kept at a minimum, since the one management, representing both interests, is able to set a just price, and in other ways to control the economic processes of the group enterprise.   In such a cooperative the production of natural wealth—to use the language of Aquinas—will be directed to a definite end, viz, the consumers' needs of a particular group in the city.   In

---

[66]Cf. *above,* IV, 4,

[67]Cf. *Farm Tenancy Report,* p. 13.

[68]Cf. Leo XIII, *Rerum Novarum,* in Husslein, *Social Well-Springs,* p. 194.

[69]Such, for example, would be a milk cooperative whose policies were set by a board composed of an equal number of representatives of those who produce—the farmers—and those who consume—the city residents.   Cooperatives of this type exist in Sweden.

this manner the city can attain to a good measure of self-sufficiency in those agricultural products that are conveniently produced within its territory, saving its transportation facilities for those products that are not.[70] Inasmuch as human energy and natural resources are consumed in transporting produce, useless transportation charges should not be added to the cost of food simply because the traffic will bear them.

5. PRODUCTION FOR USE

Throughout this study much emphasis has been placed upon the need for a definitive goal for wealth-getting: in other words, production should be for use. The truth of this principle underlies the recommendation of a certain measure of self-sufficiency for the rural family, the rural community, the city-country unit. To the degree that the family can be self-sufficient in procuring its own foodstuffs, to that degree its wealth-getting production will be directed to, and limited by a definite goal—the needs of the household. In like manner, the needs of the community and of the city will constitute immediate goals of production. This multiplication of autonomous units will tend to subordinate economic activity to an instrumental rôle in the nation. The autonomous rural family, rural community, and city-country unit are institutions apt for discouraging the unbridled acquisitive spirit. This thought seems to stand behind the proposal of Professor Tawney to organize society on a basis of function:

> It is obvious, indeed, that no change of system or machinery can avert those causes of social *malaise* which consist in the egotism, greed, or

---

[70]United Nations Food Conference, Hot Springs, Va., May, 1943, *Report*, recommends that "milk, fruits and vegetables, being perishable and expensive to transport and store, should be produced on areas adjacent to consuming centers." in *St. Paul Pioneer Press*, May 30, 1943.

quarrelsomeness of human nature. What it can do is to create an environment in which those are not the qualities which are encouraged. It cannot secure that men live up to their principles. What it can do is to establish their social order upon principles to which, if they please, they can live up and not live down. It cannot control their actions. It can offer them an end on which to fix their minds.[71]

In a society where production of agricultural products for autonomous social groups has given way to a more centralized production, it follows of necessity that there will be an increase of such charges upon society as those of transportation, processing, storage and distribution. These charges explain the very great spread between the cost of production and the consumer price.[72] In our acquisitive society,[73] born of economic liberalism, there are no criteria by which to judge whether such charges upon society as those entailed in the distribution of food are desirable or not. For it follows as a corollary, from the recognition of the pursuit of riches for their own sake, "that all economic activity is equally estimable, whether it is subordinated to a social purpose or not."[74] Consequently, if traffic will bear increased distribution costs—whether in transportation, or advertising, or in added handling or processing—then the

---

[71]Tawney, R. H., *The Acquisitive Society*, pp. 180-1.

[72]According to the study of the Twentieth Century Fund, *Does Distribution Cost Too Much?*, N.Y.: Twentieth Century Fund, 1939, p. 26, the distribution of most raw food stuffs...costs more than their production. Four cents out of every five paid by consumers for such bulky perishables as cabbage, carrots, and celery, goes to distributors, and only one cent to farmers. For processed foods a very complex process intervenes between producer and consumer: "bread and cereals all sell at retail prices which are from 143 to 975 per cent higher than the farm value of the wheat or rye from which they are made. Canned foods on the whole, show even greater spreads." p. 31.

[73]Cf. Pius XII, "1942 Christmas Message," in *Catholic Mind*, XLI: 961, Jan., 1943, p. 48.

charges are by this fact already justified.[75] Since society must meet these charges, even though they may not be for the common good, hardships will inevitably result. A re-emphasis upon production for use—whether by a family or a community, or a city—will provide a teleological principle for the limitation and direction of agricultural production and of trafficking in agricultural products.[76]

6. THE CONTEMPORARY SHIFT TO NON-AGRICULTURAL OCCUPATIONS

St. Thomas, it will be recalled, regarded the securing of wealth from plants and animals as a natural form of wealth-getting, and one that was praiseworthy.[77] The teaching of the Physiocrats that agriculture alone yields a

---

[74]Tawney, R. H., *op. cit.*, p. 33.

[75]This appears to be the philosophy of the authors of the Twentieth Century Fund *Report*, who write: "the fact that it may cost five times as much to get cabbages into consumers' hands as it does to grow them originally, does not necessarily indicate that there are any legitimate grounds for complaint. In such a case, growing is relatively simple and inexpensive compared with transportation and marketing." p. 346. Cf., also, Waring, James M. S., "Panics, Panaceas and Principles." in *Thought*, XVIII: 69, June, 1943, p. 233.

[76]Msgr. Fulton J. Sheen, *Freedom Under God*, Milwaukee: Bruce, 1940, pp. 259-60, writes that "it is this emphasis on exchange value, to the utter forgetfulness of use value which has brought on the peculiar modern paradox of starvation amidst plenty...Liberty resides more in use value than in exchange value. The American system originally was founded on the use value of agriculture because a man who lives on land is less dependent than a man who lives on the market." Schmiedeler, Edgar, N.C.W.C. pamphlet, *Balanced Abundance*, N.Y.: Paulist Press, 1937, p. 7, seeking for an explanation for the low standard of living in some sections of our population finds that a leading cause is the emphasis on the profit motive in economic life.

[77]Cf. *above*, chap. IV, sect. 2, c.

produit net is in this same tradition of thought.[78]   It was
the conviction of Jefferson that cultivators should not be
taken from the soil.[79]

The practice in this country has not been in accord with
this emphasis upon natural wealth-getting. The history
of the last six or seven decades records a great shifting
among the gainful workers away from agriculture and the
extractive industries (natural wealth-getting).[80] The shift
was particularly in favor of trade and transportation,
clerical, professional and public service.[81] Several factors
have been influential in this regard. There has been a
notable increase in the agricultural production per person
employed.[82] Again, the law of diminishing returns would

---

[78]Quesnay, *Oeuvres*, Oncken ed., p. 331, Maximes Générales no.
III, lays it down as a maxim that "le souvrain et la nation ne per-
dent jamais de vue que la terre est l'unique source des richesses, et que
c'est l'agriculture qui, les multiplie." He would allow the pursuit of
the arts and crafts and manufacturing only on the condition that they
took no capital or labor that might otherwise be used for agricultural
production.

[79]Cf. Thomas Jefferson, *Letter of Jefferson to John Jay*, August
23, 1785, quoted in Chinard, G., *Correspondence of Jefferson and Du
Pont de Nemours*, Baltimore: Johns Hopkins Press, 1931, p. XLVI:
"as long, therefore, as they (the cultivators of the earth) can find
employment in this line, I would not convert them into mariners,
artisans or anything else."

[80]Twentieth Century Fund, Report, *Does Distribution Cost Too
Much?*, N.Y.: The Twentieth Century Fund, 1939, p. 10, finds that in
1870, the total number of gainful workers in agriculture and the extractive industries was 54.9 per cent of the nation's total gainful
workers. In 1930 the total number was 23.9 per cent. Cf. also Pius
XII, *Sertum Laetitiae*, in *Principles for Peace*, N. 1463, where he lists
the flight from the land as one of the great evils of the day.

[81]Cf. Baker, Borsodi, Wilson, *Agriculture in Modern Life*, p. 30.

[82]Cf. Dummeier, E. F., and Heflebower, R. B., *Economics with
Applications to Agriculture*, N.Y.: McGraw-Hill, 1940, p. 110, who
state that the output per man was 46 per cent higher in 1928-1930
than in 1899-1901. "So effective," they write, "has been the improvement that, according to one careful student, 15 per cent of the population using the most improved methods could supply the remaining 85
per cent with food and clothing materials."

tend to favor extensive rather than intensive cultivation.[33] It is quite understandable that the individual, who seeks the greatest gain from his investment of capital and labor would conform his economic life to this law. It is quite in keeping with *laissez faire* principles that he should seek the greatest proportionate gain from his capital and labor, by employing the latter extensively over many acres rather than intensively over a few.

Without attempting a complete solution of the economic aspects of this problem, yet it is in the realm of philosophy to point out that the law of diminishing returns will, in time of necessity, be forced to cede to the demands of the common good. When it comes about that a country, by reason of the demands of its own growing population, or by reason of the demands for food from other countries of the World Commonwealth, must have greater agricultural production, then the law of diminishing returns must cede to the demand for the greatest total agricultural production possible for that country. Extensive cultivation will have to give way to intensive, in order that the total yield of the country may be increased. The concept of a world economic common good implies that our agrarian policy must take into consideration the needs of other peoples for *Lebensraum* or for additional exports from us of food and clothing materials.[34] This may necessitate a greater per-

---

[33]Marshall, Alfred, *Principles of Economics*, 8th ed., 1920, pp. 150-1, quoted by Dummeier and Heflebower, *op. cit.*, p. 97, provisionally worded this law as follows: "an increase in the capital and labour applied to the cultivation of land causes in general a less than proportionate increase in the amount of produce raised, unless it happens to coincide with an improvement in the arts of agriculture."

[34]Apropos of our world obligations Pius XI, encyclical letter, *Ubi Arcano Dei*, in *Principles for Peace*, n. 778, reminds us "that all men are our brothers and members of the same great human family, that other nations have an equal right with us both to life and to prosperity, that it is never lawful nor even wise, to dissociate morality from the affairs of practical life."

centage of our population being engaged in a more intensive production of natural wealth.[85]

Moreover, the tendency toward large scale agriculture, concomitant with the shift of the gainfully employed to non-agricultural occupations, may prove to be a short-sighted policy. In this type of agriculture the emphasis is upon cash crops for market, efficiently produced on large tracts of land, and necessitating the use of artificial fertilizers. The American commercial farmer has been called, with good reason, a soil chemist, rather than a soil biologist. In his preoccupation for a return on capital and labor he has depleted the soil.[86]   Accordingly, the shift of workers from agriculture is not to be regarded as an inevitable step, simply because it is in the direction of efficiency. Far from being an end in itself, efficiency merely enters into the selection of means. If it stands in the way of achieving the

---

[85]Were there to be a shift towards the cultivation of smaller tracts of land in this country it does not follow that the law of diminishing returns would immediately begin to operate. Dummeier and Heflebower, *op. cit.*, p. 98, list three conditions that will, according to Marshall, delay the operation of diminishing returns in agriculture: (1) improvements in the arts of agriculture, (2) such inadequate previous applications of labor and capital to land that more than a proportionate return would have been realized from increased applications, and (3) increase in skill of the individual cultivator. In this country the way is open for more extensive use of labor-saving machinery for small scale production; for the supplying of capital to our poorer agricultural regions, and for education in agricultural methods.

[86]Cf. Rawe, John C., "Biological Technology on the Land," *Catholic Rural Life Bulletin*, 2:3, August 20, 1939, p. 21, who reports the findings of the Agricultural Research Laboratories, Dornach, Switzerland. This group has criticized American commercial agriculture for mining our soil and causing it to become deficient in humus, thereby rendering it incapable of absorbing much water. Cf. also Ligutti, L. G., and Rawe, John C., *Rural Roads to Security*, Milwaukee: Bruce, 1940, p. 215, who write that, "under present low technologies of agricultural mining, we lose by the three processes of erosion over three billion tons of good soil every year."

common good, or higher personal values, then it must give way.

7. A WIDER DISTRIBUTION OF PROPERTY IN LAND[87]

The system of property defended by St. Thomas is expressed quite accurately in the formula of private ownership with community of use. The right of the private owner is not absolute and must be interpreted in terms of the common good. More specifically, St. Thomas based the validity of a man's right to a particular field upon the fact that he can cultivate it opportunely, and should be guaranteed the right to do so without molestation. This is the foundation of his private right over it. Like Aristotle, Aquinas recognizes the state's right to regulate the alienation of private property in land for the common good.[88] Aquinas' teaching on property in land is an integral part of his plans for sound socio-economic order.

a) Papal Teaching

Pope Leo XIII finds a cogent argument for private property in the fact that man, as a rational creature who has the foresight to plan for future contingencies, must have assurance that his needs can be satisfied. In the words of *Rerum Novarum*, "nature, therefore, owes to man a storehouse that shall never fail, the daily supply of his daily wants. And this he finds only in the inexhaustible fertility of the earth."[89] The argument holds for all pro-

---

[87]The question of property in land has already been touched upon in treating of the re-establishment of a strong rural domestic order. Here it will be treated in more general terms.

[88]Cf. *above*, chap. IV, sect. 6.

[89]Leo XIII, encyclical letter *Rerum Novarum*, (*The Condition of the Workingman*), 1891, in Husslein, Joseph, S.J., Milwaukee: Bruce, 1940, p. 171; *Manifesto* of the N.C.R.L.C., pp. 9-10, develops this argument as follows: "Man under present conditions of human society

ductive property, but it has special force in demonstrating the need for private property in land, from whence comes all subsistence.[90] A further argument for private property is deduced from the fact that a man, by expending his efforts upon uncultivated nature, leaves his personal imprint upon it. The development of this argument by Pope Leo XIII furnishes an interesting commentary on Aquinas' statement that a man has a right to a field because he can cultivate it opportunely. Leo XIII writes:

> Now, when man thus spends the industry of his mind and the strength of his body in procuring the fruits of nature, by that act he makes his own that portion of nature's field which he cultivates —that portion on which he leaves, as it were, the impress of his own personality; and it cannot but be just that he should possess that portion as his own, and should have a right to keep it without molestation.[91]

The papal program of social reform lays great stress on the need for a wider distribution of productive property. Explicit recommendation is made that the family be given *lebensraum* whereby it can develop to its full stature.[92]

---

needs property to provide the necessities of life for himself and for his family, to live as a free man and to achieve for himself and for his family the destiny, temporal and eternal, the Creator has intended for him." The National Committee for Alliance of Agrarian and Distributist Groups, *Report of Platform Committee*, adopted June 5, 1936, quoted by Rawe, John C., "The Agrarian Concept of Property," *Modern Schoolman*, Vol. XIV, no. 1, pp. 4-6, stands for a "wide distribution of responsible private ownership of land" as a guarantee of human freedom.

[90]Cf. Leo XIII, *loc. cit.*; Hocking, William Ernest, "A Philosophy of Life for the American Farmer (and others)," in *1940 Yearbook of Agriculture*, Washington: Government Printing Office, 1940, p. 1068, writes that "real property comes to its best expression in the farm operated by its owner or owners."

[91]Leo XIII, *op. cit.*, p. 172.

[92]Cf. *above*, sect. 1.

Comprehending in his view the needs of the whole world, Pius XII asks that uncultivated regions of the world be opened for immigration; that "the right of the family to vital space" be recognized; that there be a "more favorable distribution of men on the earth's surface, suitable to colonies of agricultural workers; that surface which God created and prepared for the use of all."[93] Leo XIII sees many advantages resulting if workmen are given the opportunity to obtain a share in the land: the gulf between vast wealth and deep poverty will be bridged; the fruits of the earth will be raised in greater abundance; and men will be more firmly settled in their country.[94]

b) The American Tradition

Mention has already been made of the fact that Jefferson hoped the United States would remain essentially an agrarian nation.[95] He believed in complete political democracy, in which all should have the vote because all should have real property. Freedom, according to his ideal, "can be approximated only in a simple agrarian world, in which self-supporting farms are supplemented by the skilled artisans of village communities."[96] The defense of private property by others among the Founding Fathers— Washington, Adams, Madison—rested upon s i m i l a r grounds. They believed that self-government went hand in hand with the wide distribution of productive property. "The expropriated man, they thought, had no power of resistance. Politically he might be a free man; but economically he was unfree."[97] Moreover, it appeared to them

---

[93]Pius XII, encyclical letter, *La Solennita della Pentecoste* (*Pentecostal Address*), 1941, in *Principles for Peace*, n. 1693.

[94]Leo XIII, *op. cit.*, pp. 194-5.

[95]Cf. *above*, chap. V, sect. 3, d.

[96]Agar, Herbert, *Land of the Free*, Boston: Houghton Mifflin, 1935, p. 41.

[97]Agar, H., *op. cit.*, p. 40.

"that widely distributed property in land must be the basis of a proprietarian society."[98]

c) The Policy Adopted in the Report of the President's Committee on Farm Tenancy

The policy of the Founding Fathers, supported both by sound philosophical reasoning and by the experience of history, has not been realized for the United States. After observing that "farmhome ownership has been approved throughout American history," the President's Committee on Farm Tenancy reports that, during the past 55 years, "there has been a continuous and marked decrease in the proportion of operating owners and an accompanying increase in the proportion of tenants."[99] Because of the striking correlation between tenancy and soil erosion, property in land has suffered. Rural community life has also suffered, because the tenant population has been a shifting population. There is a large and apparently increasing number of laborers who migrate long distances. One-fourth to one-fifth of the farm population is in extreme poverty. Many families are on submarginal land; many on holdings of inadequate size; many owners are hopelessly in

---

[98] Agar, H., *op. cit.*, p. 270. Cf. also Belloc, H., *The Restoration of Property*, N.Y.: Sheed and Ward, 1936, p. 103-4, who makes a similar observation for the entire western world. "The Restoration of Property," he writes, "means, and has meant throughout history in nearly all places and times, primarily, the restoration of property in land... Property in land...in our western world is, and has been throughout all our development, the guarantee of citizenship and the foundation thereof."

[99] *Farm Tenancy*, Report of the President's Committee, February 1937, Washington: Government Printing Office, 1937, p. 3. Tenancy has increased from 25 per cent of all farmers in 1880 to 42 per cent in 1935. In some states the equity of operating farmers in their lands is little more than one-fifth, nearly four-fifths being in the hand of landlords and mortgage holders.

debt; and many young people are unable to obtain farms.[100]

These unhealthy socio-economic conditions in contemporary rural United States are the fruits of an unsound agrarian domestic and occupational order that has left millions without a satisfactory, organic integration into the social body. The solution of this problem must include a provision for a wider distribution of private property in land as a means of rehabilitating the rural family and community. Toward this end the agrarian-decentralist movement has made valuable contributions. In like manner, the recommendations of the President's Committee on Farm Tenancy merit careful consideration, inasmuch as they express an interpretation of private property in land that is more in accord with the Thomistic thought than with the exaggerated individualistic view that has hitherto prevailed in this country.

The general aim of the President's Committee is the establishment of family-size farms, varying in size according to the families' capacity for independent management. While it recognizes that the majority of farms should be developed for full-time farming, it sees the need for a considerable number of small units for part-time farming by farm laborers and other rural workers who have outside employment.[101] It further suggests that cooperative groups ought to be aided to acquire land by purchase or long lease for subleasing to group members. This same Committee makes the significant observation in regard to this plan that "the cooperative organization would serve the function of a non-profit seeking landlord, working in the interest of its membership."[102] This suggestion is well

---

[100]*Farm Tenancy*, pp. 4-7, *passim.*

[101]To do this would be to meet the needs of those unfortunate laborers of whom Pius XI writes: "there is the immense army of hired rural laborers, whose condition is depressed in the extreme, and who have no hope of ever obtaining a share in the land." *Quadragesimo Anno*, (America Press) p. 18.

[102]*Farm Tenancy*, p. 13.

worth considering. Not only would it eliminate certain evils of landlordism but it offers a means of realizing those benefits of rural community cooperation that were enjoyed under the seigniorial organization, without binding the farmers with any degree of unfreedom. However, in the absence of this unfreedom that had characterized seigniorial organization and had given stability to its cooperative organization, it is not to be expected that the small farmers will cooperate successfully, unless they are taught through a very thorough educational program to think again in terms of the local common good, or unless they are constrained to do so by some authority.

The President's Committee offers certain plans for attaining these desirable ends. It proposes rehabilitation loans for those who urgently need financial assistance, but cannot obtain it from existing agencies, public or private. It recommends a program of land purchase by the United States Federal Government and disposition of the land under long-term—twenty to forty years—contracts of sale to operating farmers. The purchaser under these contracts, though subject to certain restrictive safeguards, would be assured a right to use (but not abuse) the land at low annual cost, to make reasonable improvements, to accumulate an equity and dispose of it at current appraised value. The important restrictive safeguard states that final payment should not be receivable until the end of the contract period.[103] By reason of this clause strong objections have been raised against the recommendations of the President's Committee, and against the Farm Security Administration, which is the agency created for the furtherance of the Committee's recommendations.[104]

---

[103]*Farm Tenancy*, p. 12.

[104]In his individual statement, as a member of the President's Committee, Edward A. O'Neal, President of the American Farm Bureau Federation, objects to this clause: "I cannot approve the principle of withholding the transfer of title to any purchaser who is able to pay the principal indebtedness for which he obligated himself at

The President's Committee justifies its stand on the ground that a rise of land values might induce farmers under purchase contract to pay off the loan, to obtain a deed, and sell all or part of the property at a profit. The objectives of the proposed program would thus be nullified; farms would fall into ownership by non-farmers and operation by tenants. Uneconomic subdivision of holdings might also result. This fear is not unwarranted. It is a fact of history that many large seigniorial landholders were unable to hold their lands against the impact of the growing money economy, and lost them through mortgaging and through the practice of farming them out for profit. When feudal tenure gave way to a system of land tenure that permitted free alienation, agrarian organization was disrupted.[105] It is to be remembered also that great hardships resulted for the small cultivator in England during the sixteenth to the eighteenth centuries when the free alienation of land, without regard for the common good, came to be accepted as a right of private property. Fee-simple ownership was in the ascendency and would countenance no restrictions. The Committee points to its harmful effects in this country:

> The land policy adopted by this country, under which title to practically all of the agricultural land of the Nation passed to private owners in fee simple absolute, has proved defective as a means of keeping the land in the ownership of those who work it. Fee-simple ownership has also implied that the right to unrestricted use was also a right to abuse of the land.[106]

---

any time that he is able to make such payment. I regard the proposed restriction on alienation of lands as contrary to sound American jurisprudence and deem it in conflict with the desired policy regarding land ownership. By and large, I am of the conviction that a man who owns a proper equity in a farm or has accumulated the amount available to own such an equity is capable of the responsibilities of such ownership." *Farm Tenancy*, p. 23.

[105]Cf. *above*, chap. II, near the end.

[106]*Farm Tenancy*, p. 6.

The Committee therefore asserts the Nation's right, using the device of federal land purchase with the retention of the title for a long period, "to discourage subdivision of economic units, wastage of natural resources, reckless speculation, and absentee landlordism and tenancy."[107]   Thomistic teaching insists that the institution of private property must be interpreted in terms of the common good, and it recognizes the right of the State to regulate the sale of land for the common good.   Accordingly, on Thomistic principles the state has the general right to prevent land abuses; and it probably has the right to place this temporary restriction upon alienation of the land that it holds, with a view to helping the small cultivator to stable ownership. This is a case where the State is affirming its rights to interpret private property in terms of the common good against those who hold to the absolute rights of fee-simple ownership.

The President's Committee further recommends a capital-gains tax, which by taking a large percentage of the unearned net increment, would materially discourage buying land merely for the purpose of early resale.[108]   It asks the individual states to regulate the landlord-tenant relations by insisting upon more satisfactory lease contracts. A differential tax favorable to the family-size owner-operated farm offers itself as a powerful weapon for stimulating an increase in the number of such farms.   The President's Committee goes on record as favoring such a tax.[109]

---

[107] *Farm Tenancy*, pp. 12-3.

[108] Cf. *Farm Tenancy*, p. 17; *Manifesto*, N.C.R.L.C., p. 189.

[109] Cf. *Farm Tenancy*, p. 18; *Manifesto*, N.C.R.L.C., 189-90, also approves such a tax: "a differential land tax providing for the exemption of homesteads with the progressive land tax is recommended primarily because of its social implications"; Ryan, John A., *Distributive Justice*, N.Y.: Macmillan, 1942, p. 78, considers it just that "every estate containing more than a maximum number of acres, or having more than a maximum total value, could be compelled to pay a special tax in addition to the ordinary tax levied on the land of the

8. CONCLUSION

To suggest that more families be established on the land where they may enjoy a measure of completeness in living, to suggest a certain self-sufficiency of life for the rural community, and a still greater measure of self-sufficiency for the city-country unit, is, undoubtedly, to go against the present determined trend of events toward centralization, and to propose a radical reformation of our economic life. It is to suggest that the modern world has complicated unduly the process of procuring the things that are necessary for the good life. The more common approach at reforming our economic life is to accept "the essentials of the economic system as it exists" and to concentrate upon finding a control for the system.[110] Yet the wisdom of the present system can well be questioned on the ground that this system has brought too much interdependence in economic affairs:

> The greatest defect is that it (the present economic system) is a system of complete and complex interdependence in the economic order. . . Such interdependence makes every economic problem a worldwide problem, every disaster a disaster of far-reaching importance.[111]

same value"; Belloc, Hilaire, *Restoration of Property*, p. 107, advocates one tax for owners on the land; another radically higher one for owners off the land.

[110]Cf. Nutting, W. D., "On Freedom and Reform; Some Agrarian Views," *Review of Politics*, 4: 432-44, October, 1942, about p. 425.

[111]Nutting, W. D., *op. cit.*, p. 435. The system is attacked on political grounds. Because of its complexity common people can have no part in directing it; nor can they have the knowledge even to select leaders who they know to be competent to direct it for them. Hence charlatans step in. Cf. also Hoffman, Ross, "The Task of Restoring Christendom," in *Thought*, XVIII: 68, March, 1943, pp. 20-1, does not think that we should accept as inevitable the continuation of the large planned, bureaucratic and semi-socialistic states, fashioned by the industrial revolution and total war.

Whatever may prove to be the future of this system it appears certain that its excessive interdependence and centralization are at variance with the thought of Aquinas; and that the counter policy of the agrarian-decentralist movement is far more in accord with it.

In his Christmas message of 1942, Pope Pius XII has singled out the basic evils in modern political and social life. In past decades the basic evil was the prevalence of a "fateful economy" during which the lives of all citizens were subordinated to the stimulus of gain. To this economy "there now succeeds another and no less fateful policy which, while it considers everybody and everything with reference to the State, excludes all thought of ethics or religion."[112] The agrarian policy outlined in this chapter, by strengthening the autonomous groups within the State —the family group on the land and the rural community— and by subjecting the complex economic processes in which the modern State finds itself deeply involved, to a natural teleological order, will do much to further the internal order and peace of the State and will save it from the necessity of imposing arbitrary order upon society from above. In such a society autonomous groups will come between State and the individual and will enable him to come to a fuller self-realization.

---

[112]Pius XII, *1942 Christmas Message,* in *Catholic Mind,* XLI: 961, pp. 48-9.

CONCLUSIONS AND RECOMMENDATIONS

According to Thomistic teleology, stressed so frequently in the course of this study, economic activity must be carried on in view of a definite end or purpose that is qualified to serve as a natural measure of its worth and as a natural principle of its limitation. Without such a limiting purpose economic activity will tend toward the ever receding goal of more wealth for its own sake. Blinded by this "enchanting vision of infinite expansion" men will forget that wealth is but a means—of which they require only a limited amount—for the good life, and they will be driven by the powerful acquisitive instinct to seek it with all their energy to the exclusion of higher values. It is not enough to hold before men an abstract scale of values expecting that this will be a satisfactory directive of their human energies, channeling them in well-proportioned amounts toward the attainment of life's diverse values. St. Thomas outlined a complete hierarchy of values. This is a necessary step in achieving order, but St. Thomas did not regard it as the only step, or as an adequate one. In a realistic manner he regarded the domestic group, the village group, the city group as necessary means of ordering, in the concrete, man's wealth-getting or economic activity. To state this in modern terminology, St. Thomas was aware of the importance of a suitable "institutional framework" for economic life. The needs of these institutions, taken individually, served as particular goals for wealth-getting. The general practice was production for use: for the use of the domestic group, the village group, the city group.

Rural life was important at the time of St. Thomas. This importance in actual practice reflected the importance of rural life in his thought, especially as this is given in his philosophy of social order and labor. From the viewpoint of labor, the husbandman held a high place. His work like that of the medical man, allowed him to use his higher faculties. Moreover, St. Thomas, along with medieval thinkers in general, held husbandry in high regard because of the purpose it filled. The wealth-getting activity *par excellence* was that carried on on the land for the immediate needs of the rural household. Wealth-getting of this kind was a natural function of the family, and in performing it the family was strengthened. Again, natural wealth-getting from the land was a most important function and principle of unity for the village group. The city group, while embracing all the functions requisite for the good life, was at the same time to be firmly rooted in its neighboring fields. As the land was fundamental for the family and the village, so St. Thomas deemed it all important that the city should be surrounded by enough land to supply its needs, rather than that it should be provisioned by merchants.

St. Thomas insured against a dissolution of these important rural institutions by his insistence that private property in land must be subject to regulations for the common good. The lord of the seigniory could not dispose of the land under his domain at will. His holding of land carried with it a responsibility for the dependent cultivators, who were guaranteed stability of tenure by the custom of the place. If there is any doubt about the efficacy, in preserving agrarian institutions, of Aquinas' teaching on property, this is dispelled in the face of the evidence furnished by the peasant evictions in England from the 16th to the 18th centuries that were made possible because men came to disregard Thomistic teaching in favor of a more individualistic view of property.

The rural life was therefore important in St. Thomas' philosophy because of its contribution to the good order of the economic, social, and political life of the State. This order is wanting today. Pius XI, in *On the Reconstruction of the Social Order*, points with regret to this fact:

The highly developed social life which once

flourished in a variety of prosperous institutions organically linked with each other, has been overthrown and all but ruined, leaving thus virtually only individuals and the State.[118]

May it not reasonably be urged that the agrarian philosophy of Aquinas be brought to bear upon our modern atomised state? The land gives stability to social institutions, and it is quite as imperative that men be well-ordered in their use of it today, as in the past.

By reason of modern technological improvements contemporary economic life is, in some of its aspects at least, unavoidably complex. Any plan to revert to the simplicity of medieval economics would be unrealistic. But there remains the possibility of restoring the teleology of medieval economics to the contemporary period. Indeed the complexity of modern economics processes makes this all the more desirable; for unless teleological principles, operating through autonomous groups within the State, give order to our highly complicated economics, the State will find itself overburdened in trying to supply by legal control what is wanting in natural control. The agrarian philosophy of Aquinas, which is an agrarian-decentralist philosophy, is of a nature to rebuild these autonomous groups—the family on the land, the rural community and the city-country unit—and it is valid today. An application of this philosophy is, of course, not the only means of reconstructing society, but it is one of those indispensable and fundamental steps which may not be ignored. This policy does not call for a rejection of legitimate economic achievements but only for a relegation to the smaller social groups of such essentially simple economic processes as the production, processing and distribution of food. This is done that the larger groups may be unhampered in the performance of other functions that they alone can perform and that are

---

[118] *Op. cit.*, p. 22, America Press edition.

required for the wider common good. This is an application of the fundamental principle of subsidiarity enunciated by Pius XI.[114] By strengthening the autonomous groups within the State, the individual will be controlled in his economic activity, protected in the pursuit of his rights, duties and legitimate personal inclinations from the encroachments of power; and the State may hope to enjoy a fortified internal order and the greater peace that is the fruit of good order.

RECOMMENDATIONS

Interpreted in terms of the contemporary *milieu* the agrarian philosophy of St. Thomas Aquinas finds expression in such practical recommendations as the following:

1. Productive property in land to more families, no other form of such property, in relation to family needs, being more conformable to nature than this. This will likely require legislation favoring the better distribution of land for the common good.

Corollary A. Productive property in land, with stability of tenure and certain other rights of private ownership, if not full ownership, to rural workers on larger farms.

Corollary B. Productive property in land to urban workers who may, through part-time farming, safeguard personal and family values while enriching the nation's standard of living through non-agricultural production in the city.

2. An increase in the number engaged part time or full time in agriculture as a means toward realizing a more careful use of the soil, as a means of securing men against the hardships resulting from a mal distribution of food, as a means of distributing more equitably and widely the bur-

---

[114]Cf. Pius XI, *On the Reconstruction of the Social Order*, America Press, p. 23.

den of feeding and clothing the people of the nation, and finally as a means of rehabilitating the laborer through dignified occupation.

3. A re-emphasis upon the rural community, enriched through the economic goods attainable through cooperative enterprise, and offering an environment favorable to the growth of political, educational and religious life, and giving to all a more personal relation to the common good.

4. A trend toward more self-sufficiency in foodstuffs for the large city as a means of simplifying the essentially simple process of food provision and as a surer guarantee of the basic necessities of life for all its inhabitants.

www.ingramcontent.com/pod-product-compliance
Lightning Source LLC
Chambersburg PA
CBHW060300290526
45789CB00001B/364